UNITY LIBRARY 8 ARCHIVES

W9-CZU-144

Praise for *Finding Faith at the Movies*

"The entertaining pastime of going to the movies is transformed into an excellent resource for spiritual formation as Mraz incorporates scripture, theology, and liturgy to underscore essential points of intersection between faith and culture." —REV. MARY E. HADDAD, Associate Rector for Formation and Worship and Facilitator of St. Bart's Goes to the Movies, St. Bartholemew's Church, New York, NY

"In *Finding Faith at the Movies*, Barbara Mraz gives us a refreshing, intelligent approach to engaging spirituality in everyday life. The connections between theology, biblical literature, and contemporary and classic films will challenge and delight the reader as well as participants in a discussion group. The depth and variety of discussion questions will lead participants to serious reflections of their own spirituality as well as encounters with classical theological principals such as suffering, sacrifice, and forgiveness. The organization is extremely helpful to the group leader and the soulful reflections will make you want to see the movies you haven't. Practical as well as inspiring." —REV. ANNE E. KITCH, Canon for Religious Education, Cathedral Church of the Nativity, Bethlehem, Pennsylvania

"Barbara Mraz offers a creative way to engage people in the art of theological reflection. She has prepared provocative materials for group study that will invite participants to bring their own experiences of twelve significant life questions into dialogue with scripture through their shared experience of a chosen movie." —THE VERY REV. DR. ANN E. P. MCELLIGOTT, Dean, St. Andrew's Cathedral, Honolulu

FINDING FAITH AT THE MOVIES

BARBARA MRAZ

Unity Library & Archives
1901 NW Blue Parkway
Unity Village, MO 64065

MOREHOUSE PUBLISHING
A Continuum imprint
HARRISBURG • LONDON • NEW YORK

Copyright © 2004 by Barbara Mraz

Morehouse Publishing
P.O. Box 1321
Harrisburg, PA 17105

Morehouse Publishing is a Continuum imprint.

2\09
MH

All rights reserved. No part of this book may be reproduced or transmitted in any form or by any means, electronic or mechanical, including photocopying, recording, or by any information storage and retrieval system, without written permission from the publisher.

Unless otherwise noted, the Scripture quotations contained in the text are from the New Revised Standard Version Bible, copyright © 1989 by the Division of Christian Education of the National Council of Churches of Christ in the USA. Used by permission. All rights reserved.

Excerpt from Eric Friesen, "Beneficiaries of an Exquisite Randomness," *Minneapolis Star-Tribune*, April 14, 1995. Reprinted by permission.

Excerpt from Christina Baldwin, *Life's Companion: Journal Writing as a Personal Quest* (New York: Bantam Books, 1991). Reprinted by permission.

Excerpt from Richard Llewellyn, *How Green Was My Valley* (New York: Laurel Publishing, 1940). Reprinted by permission.

Design by Corey Kent

Library of Congress Cataloging-in-Publication Data

Mraz, Barbara, 1944–
    Finding faith at the movies / Barbara Mraz.
        p. cm.
    ISBN 0-8192-1955-X (pbk.)
    1. Motion pictures in Christian education.   I. Title.
BV1535.4.M73 2004
268'.67--dc21

                                    2003013014

Printed in the United States of America

04 05 06 07   08 09 6 5 4 3 2 1

To St. John the Baptist Episcopal Church
MINNEAPOLIS, MINNESOTA

1-19-09 Emery-Pratt $12.95

CONTENTS

ACKNOWLEDGMENTS

Thank you to all of the movie lovers whose perceptive insights and challenging questions have helped me develop the material for this book. Appreciation is also extended to the congregation which I now serve as deacon, St. John the Evangelist Episcopal Church in St. Paul, Minnesota, for nurturing my ministry and my soul. I am also grateful for the encouragement of Debra Farrington at Morehouse and the wise counsel of Nancy Fitzgerald, the most pastoral of editors.

For unwavering support in countless ways, my deep gratitude goes to Kit Naylor with her formidable literary skills and generous heart, and to the Rev. Frank and Alys Wilson, Kristine Holmgren, Jeanne Beamish, Jim and Judi Brandt, Rex and Linda McKee, Audrey Saxton, Patricia Johnston, Malcolm McDonald, and Connie and Bob Schmitz.

And to my darlings Emily, Anna, Ottar, and to Jeanne Blake—lifelong Best Friend—not a day goes by when I don't thank God you are in my life.

ACKNOWLEDGMENTS

INTRODUCTION

This book is for you if:

You are a group leader who wants a friendly guide to using films in Christian education. Or . . .

You are a person who loves movies and are interested in using them individually or with friends as a way of exploring and enriching your faith.

Commercial, feature-length films are a gold mine for learning about theology, discussing spiritual questions, and bridging the gap between the church and the world. This book makes it easy for you to use Hollywood films efficiently and effectively as a way of exploring Christian faith.

A common problem in using films in a class or a group is that often people don't want to spend two hours in church watching a film and then discussing it. Sunday-morning between-services time slots, for example, are often only an hour long, so watching an entire movie is impossible, and week-to-week carryover can be awkward. Similarly, evening programs that consume two hours viewing a film frequently end up shortcutting discussion.

This book takes a different approach. It shows you how to focus on one major story line from a movie, allowing you and the group to view—and discuss—a feature-length film in a variety of settings and time frames. After class, many people may choose to rent the movie being discussed and watch it in its entirety at home. This book can also be a helpful resource for them.

For each movie, you'll find the following:

1. A theological theme that presents the film in terms of a key question of faith.
2. Guidelines for selecting and using a film, including cautionary notes and realistic advice regarding which films would work best in a particular group.
3. Background material on the film, including a synopsis of the story and a reflective essay that elaborates on the theme in the context of the film.
4. DVD and VCR numbers indicating which scenes to show to make both the film and the discussion fit into a one-hour time slot. Transitional material to bridge the scenes is also provided.
5. Scriptural passages that relate to the film.
6. Discussion questions to expand participants' thinking about the film and to relate the film to personal and spiritual issues.
7. Extension activities to continue discussion throughout the week or to encourage personal, individual reflection.

Practical Suggestions for the Group Leader

1. Watch the entire movie yourself before using it in class. This will not only give you more confidence in using the film, it will also help you answer unanticipated questions about the plot.
2. Get an assistant to run the DVD or VCR for you, so you can concentrate on presenting the material and facilitating the discussion. (A techno-wise teenager is ideal, although an able adult will do!) The assistant should be familiar with the equipment and should run through the clips ahead of time *on the equipment that will be used* to become familiar with the exact location of each film segment. The assistant can locate the next scene on the VCR or DVD while the leader provides transitional material to the group, answers questions, or leads the discussion.

    NOTE: If you have difficulty setting the VCR on zero, simply advance the tape to the starting point indicated for the film, eject the tape from the machine, and reinsert it. The VCR will now be on "0" at the appropriate point. Directions are given regarding when to stop each scene. (If you can gain access to a DVD player, this makes the whole process easier.)

3. Pick and choose among the discussion questions and the scriptural references. You might give participants the scriptural references a week ahead of time, so they can reflect on them before the next group meeting. And be flexible: feel free to add discussion questions of your own, or to explore ideas and questions raised by group members.

4. Structure your class. Here are suggestions:

   a. Present the theme and the key question for the day. (You may want to write them on the board before the group arrives.)

   b. Ask participants to read the selected scriptural lesson. Suggest that they keep this lesson in mind as they watch the specific movie excerpts.

   c. Read the "Background" section aloud to the class.

   d. Have your assistant show the designated scenes, either pausing for a brief discussion after each one or waiting until the end for discussion.

   e. Spend a few minutes getting reactions and general comments about the movie from the group. Then have the group discuss questions you have selected from the list provided.

   f. Read the "Reflection" to the group, either before or after the discussion, if time permits.

   g. Prepare to be amazed at the depth and breadth of discussion this process brings about!

Legalities

The U.S. Copyright Law of 1976 requires a license for showing commercial videos at church events. Movie videos are released "For Home Use Only," and it is illegal to show them in other settings.

However, you can get an umbrella license from the Motion Picture Licensing Corporation (MPLC) (1-800-452-8855 or www.mplc.com) who may refer you to Christian Video Licensing International (CVLI.org). The licensing period is generally one year and there is a low annual fee, based on the size of the congregation. You can be licensed over the phone by the MPLC to start showing videos immediately, and the MPLC will bill the church and send information regarding the stipulations of the license. You might check with your diocesan office or denominational headquarters, since they may have worked out discount licensing rates with CVLI.

The license covers films from nearly fifty studios. A list will be provided to you when you apply for your umbrella license. Studios are continually being added to the list; a studio not on the list now may be added later. (If a studio that owns the copyright of a film you want to show at church is not on the list, you must write directly to the producers for permission.) Before using them, you should check the current list for the status of the movies in this book.

It is illegal to copy excerpts from commercial movies onto a new tape, forming a collection of footage for use with this book. That's why the VCR settings and DVD scene numbers are provided here.

If you don't want to go the licensing route, your alternative is to ask group members to watch a video at home and discuss it at a subsequent gathering.

More information on legal issues is readily available at either website.

There are two ways of spreading light:
to be the candle
or the mirror that reflects it.

—Edith Wharton

CHAPTER 1

Sacrifice: What Do We Owe One Another?

Saving Private Ryan

DREAMWORKS, 1998, WITH TOM HANKS, MATT DAMON. WINNER OF TWO ACADEMY AWARDS, INCLUDING BEST DIRECTOR (STEVEN SPIELBERG). RATED R FOR SCENES OF WARTIME VIOLENCE.

You are not your own . . . You were bought with a price.
  –1 Corinthians 6:19–20

For the growing good of the world is partly dependent on unhistoric acts; and that things are not so ill with you and me as they might have been, is half owing to the number who lived faithfully a hidden life, and rest in unvisited tombs.
  –George Eliot, *Middlemarch*

Tips for Using This Movie

Saving Private Ryan is a potentially life-changing movie. After we've seen it, it's impossible to view World War II, the soldiers who fought in it, and our own daily lives in the same way. Yet many people avoided this film because of the thirty-minute scene near the beginning that shows the violence, brutality, and human suffering of war in graphic and horrifying detail. Although it could be argued that people should be required to sit through these scenes so that they really understand the hell that is combat, it can be deeply upsetting for many of us. The clips selected avoid the segment in question and focus instead on two of the main characters and their sense of duty to their country and their comrades. This is a brilliant film that presents questions each of us should ask ourselves every day of our lives.

For this particular movie, it is best to play all the clips in sequence before beginning the discussion, using the transitional material provided to bridge the scenes.

Background

Provide the background information that group members will need to follow the excerpts and put them into perspective by reading aloud—or adapting—this brief synopsis.

Considered by many veterans to be the most realistic and accurate movie ever made about World War II, *Saving Private Ryan* tells the story of a special patrol sent to rescue Pvt. James Ryan (Matt Damon), the last surviving son in a family of four brothers, three of whom have been killed in battle. The patrol, led by Sgt. Joe Miller (Tom Hanks), loses three of its seven soldiers in the effort to bring Private Ryan to safety. When the patrol finally finds him, the reluctant Ryan is ordered to leave his unit. On the journey back, Sergeant Miller is mortally wounded. But before he dies, he instructs Private Ryan to "Earn this," referring to the sacrifices made by the men of the patrol who saved him. The movie is bracketed at the beginning and end by two scenes in which an older James Ryan visits the cemetery in Normandy where Joe Miller is buried.

This film is a powerful stimulus to discuss two essential issues: First, how is the concept of sacrifice central to Christianity? Second, what is our duty to our neighbor?

Reflection: The Rhythms of Sacrifice

Read this selection to the group. Or, you may wish to use this reflection as a springboard to writing a reflection of your own to share with the group.

"Be grateful you have a roof over your head and three meals a day on the table," my mother preached to my brother and me. It was the 1950s, and with memories of the Great Depression still fresh in her mind, she reused aluminum foil and frequently served leftovers. She also insisted that we eat everything on our plates because there were children starving in China. "So send them this," I retorted, offering up my untouched lima beans.

Her comments generated a vague guilt, not that I had so much while others had so little, but that I didn't feel more sincerely grateful. Having food and shelter didn't seem like a big deal, since I had never *not* had them. It was the same vague guilt I felt in church on Good Friday when I heard about Jesus suffering and dying for my sins. I tried to feel truly sad about the fact that Jesus had sacrificed his life for me—but couldn't quite pull it off, especially with Easter and the Resurrection just two days away.

Yet I have often willingly, almost unthinkingly, made sacrifices for others. I have made sacrifices of all types for my children— of time, money, and emotional energy—but these things haven't felt like sacrifices. I'm happy to give them what I can, simply because I love them beyond words and want to offer them a good start in life. I've sacrificed friendships because I had no choice but to speak out about an important issue, or given up precious time because a neighbor was in trouble. Most of us willingly sacrifice without any expectation of repayment or even gratitude, though acknowledgment of our good deeds is welcome if it comes.

The concept of sacrifice is a compelling one, as is the idea of somehow living up to the complex legacy bequeathed to us by our parents' generation. "CBS News" recently noted that veterans of World War II are currently dying at the rate of a thousand a day. How rapidly what journalist Tom Brokaw calls "the greatest generation" is leaving us. But does "doing your duty" within a clear-cut scenario of good guys and bad guys (as World War II is often interpreted) oversimplify the issue? In the film—as in most armed conflicts— tremendous heroism takes place, but the cost is other human lives, the currency of war.

In many ways, *Saving Private Ryan* is a mother's story. We see Mrs. Ryan only briefly, when the military car pulls up to the farmhouse and the officers get out to give her the horrific message that three of her beloved sons have been killed in battle. As they walk toward the house, she sinks to the ground, already defeated.

Yet her one surviving son is saved because a high-ranking general morally recoils from the prospect of having to write yet another letter to that mother. His determination launches the mission to find Pvt. James Ryan and "get him the hell outta there."

Saving Private Ryan calls us to intentionally acknowledge the rhythms of sacrifice—the legacy of sacrifice that pervades our political and religious history as well as the sacrifices we make each day for others. The movie cautions us not to defer a serious moral inventory until our later years and challenges us to ask ourselves now: Am I being a good person? Am I living a good life?

Film Clips to Use for a One-Hour Class
Set VCR to zero at "Dreamworks."

1. (5 min.) Credits lead into scene of military cemetery at Normandy; the time is the present. James Ryan locates the grave he is looking for. Shot of bodies on Omaha Beach, D-Day. End after "June 6, 1944" appears on the screen.
   VCR—00:00 to 4:35   DVD—begin at Scene 1
2. (9 min.) Brief shots of bodies on Omaha Beach. War Department secretaries processing papers; high-level military officials discuss the Ryan case. End after General Marshall's promise to find Private Ryan and get him to safety.
   VCR—27:00 to 36:00   DVD—begin at Scene 5
3. (7 min.) The platoon finds Private Ryan, informs him of his three brothers' deaths, and orders him to leave his unit. Miller talks to a soldier about their mission. End after soldier says, "We all earn the right to go home."
   VCR—1:46:00 to 1:53:00   DVD—begin at Scene 14
4. (10 min.) Miller is mortally wounded; before he dies, he gives Private Ryan an order. Return to cemetery scene where movie started. Continue to end of movie.
   VCR—2:32:00 to end of movie   DVD—begin at Scene 19

Total running time: 31 minutes

Film, Faith, and Scripture

Explore with your group the connections between film, faith, and Scripture by examining what the Bible says to us about sacrifice. You may read the scripture passages from your book, or ask participants to look them up and read them to the group.

Abraham Is Asked to Sacrifice His Son (Genesis 22:1–2, 9–14)

After these things, God tested Abraham. He said to him, "Abraham!" And he said, "Here I am." He said, "Take your son, your only son Isaac, whom you love, and go to the land of Moriah, and offer him there as a burnt offering on one of the mountains that I shall show you. . . ." When they came to the place that God had shown him, Abraham built an altar there and laid the wood in order. He bound his son Isaac, and laid him on the altar, on top of the wood. Then Abraham reached out his hand and took the knife to kill his son. But the angel of the Lord called to him from heaven, and said, "Abraham, Abraham!" And he said, "Here I am." He said, "Do not lay your hand on the boy or do anything to him; for now I know that you fear God, since you have not withheld your son, your only son, from me." And Abraham looked up and saw a ram, caught in a thicket by its horns. Abraham went and took the ram and offered it up as a burnt offering instead of his son. So Abraham called that place "The LORD will provide."

The Parable of the Lost Sheep (Luke 15:3–6)

So he told them this parable: "Which one of you, having a hundred sheep and losing one of them, does not leave the ninety-nine in the wilderness and go after the one that is lost until he finds it? When he has found it, he lays it on his shoulders and rejoices. And when he comes home, he calls together his friends and neighbors, saying to them, "Rejoice with me, for I have found my sheep that was lost."

Jesus Resurrects a Mother's Only Son (Luke 7:11–15)

Soon afterward he went to a town called Nain, and his disciples and a large crowd went with him. As he approached the gate of the town, a man who had died was being carried out. He was his mother's only son, and she was a widow; and with her was a large crowd from the town. When the Lord saw her, he had compassion for her and said to her, "Do not weep." Then he came forward and touched the bier, and the bearers stood still. And he said, "Young man, I say to you, rise!" The dead man sat up and began to speak, and Jesus gave him to his mother.

Discussion Questions

Invite participants to look at how the two texts—the film Saving Private Ryan *and the Bible—inform us, as people of faith, about what sacrifice means to Christians.*

1. To what things do you feel a sense of duty? A willingness to sacrifice? Family? Friends? Country? Religion? Certain values and beliefs? Why is the concept of sacrifice central to our faith as Christians? Is there spiritual value in our sacrifices, big and small, today?

2. We've heard the phrase, "To whom much is given, much is required." What is one specific thing you've received that you feel came with an "implicit requirement"? Explain. Have you fulfilled that requirement? Think about Private Ryan and the requirement attached to his gift. How do you think it might have transformed his life?

3. God tests Abraham by asking him to sacrifice his son Isaac. What are some ways today that other forces might ask—or demand—that we sacrifice our children? How and why are children worldwide being "sacrificed" today? Is sacrifice always noble, or can it be misplaced?

4. Why is the mother so central to the story? How is her experience similar to that of Mary, the mother of Jesus? How is it similar to the story in Luke 7:12 (cited earlier in this lesson), in which Jesus resurrects the only son of the widowed mother?

5. Explain how Christian faith calls you to a sense of duty or obligation since Jesus died to "atone" for our sins. What are the parallels between our duty as people saved by the sacrifice of Jesus, and Private Ryan's duty as a man saved by the sacrifice of his friends?

Extension Activity

Imagine that you could visit the grave of a family member or a friend who has sacrificed for you. Write a letter to that person, expressing what they have given you, what you feel you owe them, and what you have paid so far on that debt.

CHAPTER 2

Truth: Can Science and Religion Coexist?

Contact

WARNER BROTHERS, 1997, WITH JODIE FOSTER AND MATTHEW MCCONAGHEY. DIRECTED BY ROBERT ZEMECKIS. RATED PG.

God of all power, Ruler of the Universe, you are worthy of glory and praise. . . . At your command all things came to be: the vast expanse of interstellar space, galaxies, suns, the planets in their courses, and this fragile earth, our island home.
–Eucharistic Prayer C, The Book of Common Prayer

Something deeply hidden had to be behind things.[1]
–Albert Einstein

Tips for Using This Movie

What a theological powerhouse this movie is! The discussion topics it presents include the relationship between faith and doubt, the nature of "truth," the alleged conflict between science and religion, and how to "prove" what you believe. Above all, *Contact* makes a case for love as the most powerful force in the universe. In the context of a compelling story about a female scientist on her own mission, the film proceeds fearlessly to examine the mysteries of the universe and of the heart.

Begin discussion by considering the film on its own terms; that is, discuss the story itself and the themes it presents. If the topic of evolution versus creationism comes up, defer it until the end of the discussion, or perhaps examine it in a separate session. Pause after each of the film clips to check if anyone has questions about the story line.

Background

Provide the background information that group members will need to follow the excerpts and put them into perspective by reading aloud—or adapting—this brief synopsis.

Based on the best-selling book by Carl Sagan (and dedicated "To Carl"), *Contact* explores the nature of truth: the evidence of science and the evidence of the heart. It traces the evolution of a scientist and a life based on verifiable facts through her deep conversion to the understanding that there are crucially important things—such as love—that depend on a kind of "proof" that science cannot provide.

Dr. Ellie Arroway (Jodie Foster) has always been on a quest to make contact with new people, new ideas, and ultimately, the cosmos. After the death of her mother, young Ellie's father gives her a telescope and encourages her to study the night sky. "If it's just us [out there]," he says, "that's a lot of wasted space."

A brilliant student, Ellie completes her Ph.D. and begins pursuing her passion: investigating the possibility of human life in space. After several years, she and her colleagues detect what they think are signals from a dead star named Vega. Mysterious "plans" are transmitted for a spacecraft that could carry a human being to Vega, and Ellie is chosen to make the journey. On the voyage, she experiences a celestial event, a kind of "baptism by beauty." Her response to the sights she sees in space: "Beauty . . . No words. They should have sent a poet." She also visits a mystical place where she meets her father again, years after his death. These experiences change her to the core.

Upon her return to Earth, she learns that her space capsule malfunctioned and never left the ground. But she insists that what happened to her is true, though she has no scientific evidence to support this conclusion. Federal investigations of the Vega incident ensue, and Ellie testifies before a high-ranking committee of scientists about what she experienced. Ellie the scientist is in the embarrassing position of having to rely on standards of truth other than scientific, but is vehement that something happened to her that was real and true and changed her forever. She comes close to acknowledging that the reality of love is not provable by scientific standards, but is the most real thing in the world. Later, the investigators discover that evidence in the spacecraft confirms part of Ellie's story.

Reflection: The Heart's Truth

Read this selection to the group. Or, you may want to use this reflection as a springboard to writing your own reflection to share with the group.

The former governor of Minnesota, Jesse Ventura (previously a professional wrestler), once commented that religion was for the weak-minded. It was fine for other people, he said, but personally he didn't need it.

Outrageous as this statement is, most of us know what it's like to be misunderstood because of our faith, to be labeled as anti-intellectual, naive souls who lack evidence for their beliefs. At best, wishful thinkers.

Yet even the most hardcore agnostics and atheists have had personal moments of crisis when their staunch beliefs in science, in verifiable facts and proof as the standard for truth, crumble. Science is of little comfort when we lose someone we loved beyond words, when we receive a frightening medical diagnosis, or when loneliness threatens to overwhelm us. These situations are matters of the heart and soul. When we hit the wall, spirituality and religion may be all that is left to provide any meaning or hope for our lives, and any protection against bitterness and despair.

What about the challenge to "prove" the existence of God? The great scholar of comparative religion, Huston Smith, explains that this is impossible simply because proof requires controlled experiments and verifiable evidence.[2] If the subject of our experimentation is, by definition, a power greater than ourselves, all of the variables are not within our control.

But perhaps we know more than we realize, more than we are willing to admit. Most of us have experienced an unbelievable coincidence, a strong intuition that later proves to be true, or feelings of awe and wonder at the birth of a child or a sense of peacefulness after the good and timely death of a loved one.

Recently, I went to my eighty-three-year-old aunt's funeral. She was a restrained and formal woman who chose to live her entire life within a one-block area of the city, a nervous life of caretaking and caution ended by a difficult illness. As we walked away from the grave site to our car on that beautiful sunny morning, I looked overhead and saw a single hawk, flying high above the trees in the cloudless September sky, circling, soaring, unrestrained and free. Immediately, the thought came to my mind that this was Alyce's spirit, released and joyful, beyond the bonds of the earthly obligations and duties that had defined her life.

For a few seconds, this image brought me a palpable feeling of calm happiness and joy—until my rational side dismissed it, largely, I think, out of fear of being ridiculous. Frederick Buechner observes that we often dismiss such moments as though nothing had really happened. He concludes, "To go on as though something has happened even though we are not sure what it was or just where we are supposed to go with it, is to enter that dimension of life that religion is a word for."[3]

At one point in the film, Ellie the scientist is asked if she loved her father. She replies that of course she did. "Prove it," her accuser challenges. She insists that she cannot, but that her love for him is absolutely, without question, true. The implicit conclusion is that truth can be found in the depth of our feelings as much as in a scientific formula, and perhaps more so.

Contact draws our attention to the immensity of the universe that surrounds us, reminding us that our Earth-centered perspective is limited, if not flawed. Using the language of the camera, the scope of God extends from a micro-close-up of the tiniest cell in our bodies all the way back to the widest shot possible of the planets, stars, sun, and moons of the universe. This is the gargantuan stage on which we play out our parts in the divine plan. This is the vast domain of the Creator and Sustainer of life.

Theologian Matthew Fox writes about the 1969 Apollo mission when astronaut Rusty Schweikert, connected to the spacecraft by an umbilical cord, was left alone to float in space for several minutes. Fox notes, "During this time, Rusty had two profound conversion experiences. . . . He looked back at Mother Earth, 'a shining gem against a totally black backdrop,' and realized everything he cherished was on that gem—his family and land, music and human history with its folly and its grandeur. He was so overcome that he wanted to 'hug and kiss that gem like a mother does her firstborn child.'"[4]

When we put the world, "our island home," onto the map of the vast expanse of space, our own lives not visible even as a pinprick, and then realize that the Spirit who created and sustains it all also sees into the depths of our own hearts, our concept of God is enlarged and changed forever.

Film Clips for a One-Hour Class
Set VCR to zero at "Warner Brothers."

1. (5 min.) Ellie is a respected scientist, working with her team in New Mexico on detecting signals from space. After several years, she hears something. Stop after Ellie yells, "We've got to be sure about this."
    VCR—36:00 to 41:00   DVD—begin at Scene 11

2. (4 min.) Ellie is before a committee of scientists as a candidate to make the trip to Vega; she is asked if she believes in God. End after she puts the necklace in Palmer's hand.
    VCR—1:23:00 to 1:27:00   DVD—begin at Scene 25

3. (2 min.) (Note the DVD sequence for clips two and three is intentionally out of order.) Ellie and Josh debate the existence of God. Stop after Josh gets a call from the White House and leaves the party.
    VCR—1:13:00 to 1:15:00   DVD—begin at Scene 21

4. (17 min.) Ellie is on her way to Vega in the spacecraft. After a series of intense, violent, and jolting events (Ellie refers to them as "wormholes"), she awakens to scenes of celestial beauty. She meets her father, who gives her information about her journey. Ellie's spacecraft returns to Earth, but she is told the craft never left the ground. In the last scene, two investigators look more closely at the "evidence." End after "That is interesting, isn't it?"
    VCR—1:58:00 to 2:18:00   DVD—begin at Scene 34

Total running time: 28 minutes

Film, Faith, and Scripture

> *Explore with your group the connections between film, faith, and Scripture by examining what the Bible says to us about the relationship between science and faith. You may read the scripture passages from your book, or ask participants to look them up and read them to the group.*

God Creates the Universe (Genesis 1:1)

In the beginning when God created the heavens and the earth, the earth was a formless void and darkness covered the face of the deep, while a wind from God swept over the face of the waters.

God Makes the Two Great Lights (Genesis 1:16)

God made the two great lights—the greater light to rule the day and the lesser light to rule the night—and the stars.

The Wise Men Follow a Star (Matthew 2:9–10)

When they had heard the king, they set out; and there, ahead of them, went the star that they had seen at its rising, until it stopped over the place where the child was. When they saw that the star had stopped, they were overwhelmed with joy.

On Evidence and Proof (Proverbs 12:17)

Whoever speaks the truth gives honest evidence . . . .

Jesus Gives Proof (Acts 1:3)

After his suffering he presented himself alive to them by many convincing proofs, appearing to them during forty days and speaking about the kingdom of God.

Rabbinic Saying

Lord, do not let me use my reason against the truth . . . .

Discussion Questions

Invite participants to take a look at how the two texts—the film Contact *and the Bible—inform us, as people of faith, about the ways that both science and religion lead us to the truth.*

1. What simple, universally accepted scientific principles do we accept without question (gravity, earth revolving around the sun, DNA, etc.)? (Note to leader: Avoid a discussion of evolution at this point!)
2. What is the basis of the scientific method of proof (for example, observation, hypothesis, replication, etc.)? Science can explain so many things about our universe—but not everything. What are things you believe in deeply that you cannot scientifically or rationally prove to be true?
3. What is your "evidence" for your belief or nonbelief in God? Do you agree with the sources in the reflection that experiments to "prove" or "disprove" the existence of God are pointless? Why or why not?
4. Describe a time or place when you have been embarrassed to be a person of religious faith—when you felt it was unintellectual, unscientific, or naive to be a Christian. (Leader: Try to keep a tight rein on this question or discussion might stray far from the point.)
5. When asked what question she would ask any alien life form, Ellie replies, "How did you survive your technological adolescence without destroying yourselves?" How is our world today in its "technological adolescence"? In what way could the rapid advance of technology destroy what is important to us about our lifestyle and values?
6. What are some times in your own life when your heart has overruled your head? What truths were you responding to? Looking back, what do you think the experience shows you about your faith?
7. Recent discoveries have offered well-reasoned and carefully researched theories about the origins of life (chaos theory, the big bang, cloning, etc.). How do any of these theories complement—or clash with—your religious beliefs?

8. In what ways are Vega and the Christmas star similar? How was the function of each similar? Does the idea of the people eagerly following Vega enhance your understanding of the Epiphany?

Extension Activity

Encourage those who are interested in pursuing a discussion of creationism and evolution to watch the film *Inherit the Wind* (based on the Scopes "Monkey Trial"). The courtroom scenes, where the forces of biblical literalism and scientific liberalism go head to head, may be especially relevant. There are two versions available; the one starring Spencer Tracy is clearly superior to the remake.

CHAPTER 3

Memory: How Are Memories Vehicles of Grace?

A River Runs Through It

COLUMBIA PICTURES, 1992, WITH CRAIG SHEFFER, BRAD PITT, TOM SKERRIT. DIRECTED AND NARRATED BY ROBERT REDFORD. RATED PG.

"This is my body, which is given for you. Do this in remembrance of me."
  –Luke 22:19

The secret of redemption lies in memory.
  –Rabbinic Saying

Tips for Using This Movie

If I had to make a list of my three favorite movies of all time, this film would be on it. It offers a well-rendered presentation of an earlier historical period; family complexities honestly portrayed; stunning natural scenery; and the wise, tender voice of the narrator, remembering his rich and complicated life with eloquence and warmth. This film will evoke strong feelings in young and old, in men and women, in the hurting and in the healed.

Show all of the film clips, using the transitional material provided, before beginning the discussion.

Background

To provide a context for the excerpts and to help participants follow the movie line, read this background information to the group.

A haunting and poetic tribute to the importance of family and the healing power of memory, *A River Runs Through It* uses fly fishing as a metaphor for human life, emphasizing the importance of being attuned to God's rhythms. The film is based on a memoir of the same name by writer Norman MacLean, whose compelling words, read by actor and director Robert Redford, provide the voice-over that gives the film much of its emotional and spiritual depth.

The film begins with MacLean's enchanted childhood in the Missoula, Montana, of the 1930s, a pristine land of mountains, evergreens, and trout-filled streams and rivers. MacLean and his brother Paul are the children of a Presbyterian minister and his wife, upright, restrained, yet loving parents. The minister schools his young sons in the three-part rhythm that is the basis of proper fly fishing, as well as in prayer and Bible study. The boys conclude that "all of Jesus' disciples who were fishermen must have been fly fishermen."

Norman, the older brother, eventually goes to Dartmouth College, marries, and takes a job at the University of Chicago teaching English. Along with his wife and children, he makes frequent trips home to Missoula to see his family and go fly fishing with his brother Paul and their father.

Paul, the younger brother, stays in Missoula and becomes a newspaperman, gregarious and charming, captivating his friends and family with his good looks, outrageous stories, and superb fishing skills. Problems with gambling and alcohol, however, ravish him, and ultimately prove to be the means of his destruction while he is still in his twenties.

Paul's father is devastated by his death, but ever the dutiful Scot, goes forward bravely in his life and ministry. In one of his last sermons, clearly referring to Paul without naming him, he concludes that often, those we are closest to most elude us, but "we can still love them. We can love completely, without complete understanding."

The film ends with MacLean as an old man, alone now and still fishing the Montana streams, remembering the richness of his life, the preciousness of those he has loved, and his belief that eventually all things merge into one, and "a river runs through it."

Reflection: The Peace

Read this selection to the group. Or, you may wish to use this reflection as a springboard to writing a reflection of your own to share with the group.

It is All Saints' Sunday at the church I serve, and parishioners are bringing in photographs of people they have loved and lost—parents, grandparents, children, friends, even pets. Before the service starts, they place these pictures on tables set up near the altar and on the sills beneath the stained-glass windows running along both sides of the church. As the service begins, these photographs surround the congregation, beloved faces of the past now a part of the community gathered there, all merging into the Communion of Saints. Through this ritual, memories are blessed and sanctified, and the veil between past and present is nearly transparent.

Memory can be drawn upon to put our individual lives into a profound context of history and tradition. In his novel about a Welsh coal mining family in the late 1800s, *How Green Was My Valley*, Richard Llewelyn illustrates the power of memory and imagination:

> I saw behind me those who had gone, and before me, those who are to come. I looked back and saw my father, and his father, and all our fathers, and in front to see my son, and his sons, and the sons upon sons beyond.
> And their eyes were my eyes.
> As I felt, so they had felt, and were to feel, as then, so now, as tomorrow and forever. Then I was not afraid, for I was in a long line that had no beginning, and no end . . . I was of them, they were of me, and in me, and I in all of them.[5]

I take strength from the memories of my great-grandparents, homesteading on the Dakota prairie, from historical figures like

Eleanor Roosevelt, from my parents' stories about surviving the Depression, and even from my own previous accomplishments and resilience. Remembering can be life-giving, bequeathing to us not only a sense of our small but unique place on the continuum of human history, but also the courage to go forward.

Of course, memories can be painful, opening wounds that we hoped were healed. Sometimes, we must try to forget and simply move on with our lives, leaving the pain of our past in the hands of God.

Nowhere is the concept of memory more central than in religious faith. In Christianity, there is a continuous interplay between historical faith—as recorded in Scripture by the people who witnessed and recorded biblical events—and our own daily experiences of God. Part of the religious life is relating scriptural accounts to the events of our own lives, and in so doing, forging a concept of a personal deity.

This can be a lifelong task, since the presence of God is often most apparent in retrospect, in memory, when it becomes clear to us that at certain critical points we have indeed been directed, comforted, protected, and even saved by God, present every bit as much now as in earlier times. Can our own experiences have as much validity as those recorded two thousand years ago? A seminary professor I know once asserted, "All centuries are equidistant from God." This seems reasonable, since the alternative would be to accuse God of historical favoritism, possessing less intense concern for his children living now than for those who lived in the first century and before.

The mandate to remember appears often in Scripture. God emphasizes that he remembers his covenant with Abraham, with Isaac, with Joseph, and with Noah. He remembers his covenant with Israel. Jesus sometimes becomes impatient when his disciples do not remember his words or his miracles. We are warned not to forget the teachings of Scripture, or to pray. It seems that one of the main things God expects of us is not to forget what is truly important.

At the Last Supper, Jesus makes a simple request: that we remember him. It's an intensely personal appeal, something we'd ask of a beloved friend at the time of our death or parting. Joan Chittister once said that Jesus is imploring us to literally *re-member*, to realign the priorities and various elements of our lives within the strength, comfort, and hope that is held out to us, specifically in the Eucharist.

In *A River Runs Through It,* Norman MacLean, an old man now, recalls the story of his family. He reminds us that nothing lasts forever, except in memory. Instead of being a sad conclusion, it's an empowering one because of what the past can offer us: a context for our own struggles, a dose of courage, and healing insight into ourselves and those we have loved and lost. It is perhaps for this reason that the ancient rabbis taught that "memory and hope belong together."

Scenes to Use for a One-Hour Class
Set VCR to zero at "Columbia Pictures."

1. (9 min.) Opening credits setting the scene for the story; introduction of Mr. MacLean and his family; MacLean teaches the boys about writing and fishing; Paul and Norman go fishing. End after shots of boys throwing rocks in water, fishing in silhouette.

    VCR—00:00 to 9:00   DVD—begin at Scene 1

2. (9 min.) Norman returns home after college and graduate school and is interrogated by his father about his future plans; Norman reconnects with his brother who has become a newspaperman and a superb fisherman. End after "My brother had become an artist."

    VCR—31:00 to 40:00   DVD—begin at Scene 9

3. (12 minutes) The men go fishing together; Paul's death; Mr. MacLean reflects in the pulpit. Closing soliloquy goes through the end of the film.

    VCR—1:48:00 to end of film   DVD—begin at Scene 26

Total running time: 30 minutes

Film, Faith, and Scripture

Explore with your group the connections between film, faith, and Scripture by examining what the Bible says to us about the thread of memory that runs through our personal and communal faith. You may read the scripture passages from your book, or ask participants to look them up and read them to the group.

God Will Remember His Covenant with Noah (Genesis 9:12–17)

God said, "This is the sign of the covenant that I make between me and you and every living creature that is with you, for all future generations: I have set my bow in the clouds, and it shall be a sign of the covenant between me and the earth. When I bring clouds over the earth and the bow is seen in the clouds, I will remember my covenant that is between me and you and every living creature of all flesh . . . that is on the earth."

God Will Remember His Covenant with Jacob (Leviticus 26:42)

". . . then will I remember my covenant with Jacob; I will remember also my covenant with Isaac and also my covenant with Abraham, and I will remember the land."

Jesus Reminds His Disciples to Remember (Mark 8:17–21)

Jesus said to them, "Why are you talking about having no bread? Do you still not perceive or understand? Are your hearts hardened? Do you have eyes, and fail to see? Do you have ears, and fail to hear? And do you not remember? When I broke the five loaves for the five thousand, how many baskets full of broken pieces did you collect?" They said to him, "Twelve." "And the seven for the four thousand, how many baskets of full pieces did you collect?" And they said to this, "Seven." Then he said to them, "Do you not yet understand?"

The Injunction to Remember the Words of Jesus (Acts 20:35)

In all this I have given you an example that by such work we must support the weak, remembering the words of the Lord Jesus, for he himself said, "It is more blessed to give than to receive."

Discussion Questions

Invite participants to take a look at how the two texts—the film A River Runs Through It and the Bible—inform us, as people of faith, about the importance of memory in leading us closer to God.

1. Describe a single memory of your earlier life that has, without question, influenced who you are today. How has that memory comforted, strengthened, or sustained you in difficult times?
2. What painful memories have you had to come to terms with? Has your religious faith helped you to heal? If so, in what ways?
3. If your own family history were made into a story, what memories would comprise its major theme? Resilience? Perseverance? Hard work? Destructive patterns? Other?
4. So far, what has been the theme of your life story? Has this been similar to or different from the themes of your family's story? How does remembering past events in your personal story strengthen—or weaken—your relationship with God and others?
5. How was Mr. MacLean able to transform painful memories into healing and peace? Describe a time in your life when good memories have, over time, erased a sense of profound loss for you. How do you think God was acting in this transformation?
6. In Rev. MacLean's sermon after Paul's death, he says it is often those we are closest to who most elude us. Who is a person close to you who "eluded you" or rejected your help? What has been your response? What insight does the film offer regarding these situations?
7. How is Mr. McLean's need to remember the rich and varied events of his life related to the need of Jesus' followers to remember him in the breaking of the bread in Acts of the Apostles? What gifts does the act of remembering bring to you?

Extension Activities

Ponder your response to discussion question one, then write a detailed description of the memory you have chosen—including the sights, sounds, and visual details that are part of your remembrance. You may want to make this a regular journaling practice. You may also use this piece to accompany pictures in a family history or photo album.

CHAPTER 4

Temptation: What Are the Things That Seduce Us?

Quiz Show

HOLLYWOOD PICTURES, 1994, WITH RALPH FIENNES, JOHN TURTURRO. DIRECTED BY ROBERT REDFORD; ACADEMY AWARD NOMINATIONS FOR BEST PICTURE AND BEST DIRECTOR. RATED PG-13.

No testing has overtaken you that is not common to everyone. God is faithful, and he will not let you be tested beyond your strength, but with the testing he will also provide the way out so that you may be able to endure it.
    –1 Corinthians 10

I want! I want!
    –William Blake

Tips for Using This Movie

This film provides an excellent vehicle to approach the biblical concept of "temptation" and relate it to personal experience. It is, for the most part, a historically accurate and chilling precursor to the culture of dishonesty and sleaze that pervades much of American society today.

While this is a complicated movie, the story line that is pulled out in the excerpts provides an easy-to-follow and dramatic tale of an intelligent and good man tempted beyond his limits, and the resulting fallout affecting his family, the country, and himself. Many viewers will remember the actual events on which this movie is based.

The "Reflection" piece in this section expands the discussion of temptation beyond biblical frames of reference into the contemporary realm of the tempting choices that confront us each day.

Background

To provide a context for the excerpts and to help participants follow the movie, read this background information to the group.

The television quiz-show scandals erupted in the 1960s, when the influence of this still-new medium was expanding into all walks of life. Unlike today, trust in television and its message was high and skepticism was low; Americans were willing to believe TV as long as it entertained them. The intense and dramatic competition each week on shows such as *Tic Tac Dough, The $64,000 Question,* and *Twenty-One* attracted large viewing audiences and was the subject of animated viewer discussion throughout the week. The contestants became celebrities—as long as they kept winning. At the same time, the pressure on producers to keep creating programs that attracted large audiences and wealthy sponsors grew.

The story of *Quiz Show* is based in part on actual events that occurred on the wildly popular show *Twenty-One.* Herbert Stempel, an unattractive, brainy underdog, has a significant string of wins until producers think viewers have become tired of him. They bring in Mark Van Doren, a young, good-looking college instructor with a perfect family pedigree. They persuade Stempel to throw a round, and Van Doren wins. After initial resistance, Van Doren gives in to the temptation of continued winning, accepting explicit clues about what each week's questions will be. He becomes caught up in the glamour and status that accompanies his new role, and the farther it goes, the harder it is to stop. Finally, before a congressional committee investigating the quiz shows, Van Doren confesses what he's done and admits that he's "flown too high on borrowed wings."

Reflection: The Temptations

Read this selection to the group. Or, you may wish to use this reflection as a springboard to writing a reflection of your own to share with the group.

Temptation, guilt, and repentance are often trivialized in our culture. Look no further than the buffet line or the dessert tray.

In the faculty room of the school where I work, a large round table near the coffee pot is the site of regular crises of conscience and occasions for sin, as well as for self-imposed penance. It is the ominous goodie table. Especially during fall and early winter, in the wake of multiple holiday celebrations, it may be laden with miniature Snickers® bars from someone's Halloween leftovers; delicious assortments of bagels, bars, and muffins generously provided by parents for the faculty as a Thanksgiving treat; half of a decadent chocolate cake left over from a teacher's home birthday party, brought in "to get it out of the house"; glimmering cookies that preview a secretary's Christmas baking.

These luscious items are not devoured without the requisite apologies, mandatory confessions of sinfulness, and promises to repent and atone for caloric transgressions—statements that seem especially "spiritual" since they are usually made to no one in particular, almost whispered as prayer.

First, sorrow is expressed as the table first comes into view:
"Oh no . . . just when I thought it was safe to come in here . . ."
"Don't they know I'm weak?"

Then temptation overcomes the best of intentions:
"I'm just going to take this tiny little corner with no frosting on it . . ."
"What the heck, life is short."

Finally, penance is assigned:
"I'm not going to eat dinner tonight and I'll probably skip lunch, too."
"January 1st and it's diet city."

To well-fed Americans, food has become the occasion for sin, the enemy, evil incarnate in a slice of cheesecake. For many of us, abundance is commonplace and we have the added pounds and guilty consciences to show for it.

Ironically, while we worry about eating an extra cookie, our response to larger issues—such as the discrepancy between the lives of the poor and the rich, the proliferation of rage and hatred, and the crippling social inequities in our country and in the world—is often indifference.

Foundational biblical stories about temptation aren't always interpreted consistently. When discussing the story of Adam and Eve in my women's studies class, students wonder whether Eve, who used her God-given curiosity and in that sense was more fully human than Adam, was "framed." Did the serpent approach Eve because she seemed the weaker of the two—or the smarter? One person quipped that the fall of humankind is linked to the classic problem women have with food—and Eve's inability to stick to her eating plan!

We live in a culture that inflates desire through the media, then offers immediate and accessible means of gratification—all the credit cards we can fit in our wallets, entertainment available 24/7, and technology that makes things easier and faster. And yet the most important prayer in the Christian faith, the one we repeat each Sunday, asks God to "lead us not into temptation." As if it's God who does the leading!

Our own temptations may not fit neatly into the categories of the "Seven Deadly Sins." They may not have classical names such as pride, sloth, or lust. Rather than inflating our own importance, our temptation may be to minimize it, worrying relentlessly if we have become "all that we can be."

Mark Van Doren cannot withstand the temptations placed before him. His explanation for his actions, while an honest admission of guilt, is phrased in language that is elegant, poetic, and charming. In a culture that trivializes temptation, our own rationalizations for our sins of commission and omission may be equally ambivalent.

Scenes to Use for a One-Hour Class
Set VCR to zero at "Hollywood Pictures" logo.

1. (4 min.) The producers of *Twenty-One* propose a deal to Mark Van Doren for his appearances on their show. End after producer says, "Why would a guy like that want to be on a quiz show?"

    VCR—17:00 to 21:00   DVD—begin at Scene 6

2. (6 min.) Van Doren defeats Herb Stempel, champion for several weeks, who has been persuaded by the producers (with promises regarding his own TV future) to throw the round. Van Doren is only asked questions the producers know he can answer. End after Stempel and Van Doren shake hands.

    VCR—30:00 to 36:00   DVD—begin at Scene 8

3. (7 min.) Van Doren, unable to live with the guilt any longer, loses on purpose and gets a surprise consolation prize from the network. End after emcee Jack Barrie says, "Congratulations, Charlie."

    VCR—1:24:00 to 1:31:00   DVD—begin at Scene 20

4. (4 min.) In his apartment, Van Doren defends his ethical choices to Dick Goodwin, the lawyer sent to investigate the quiz shows. End after Goodwin says, "Don't make me call you."

    VCR—1:34:00 to 1:38:00   DVD—begin at Scene 21

5. (6 min.) Van Doren testifies before the congressional committee and suffers the consequences. End as Van Doren and his family exit the hearing room.

    VCR—1:58:00 to 2:04:00   DVD—begin at Scene 27

Total running time: 27 minutes

Film, Faith, and Scripture

Explore with your group the connections between film, faith, and Scripture by examining what the Bible says to us about temptation. You may read the scripture passages from your book, or ask participants to look them up and read them to the group.

Eve Is Tempted by the Serpent (Genesis 3:1–7)

Now the serpent was more crafty than any other wild animal that the Lord God had made. He said to the woman, "Did God say, 'You shall not eat from any tree in the garden'?" The woman said to the serpent, "We may eat of the fruit of the trees in the garden; but God said, 'You shall not eat of the fruit of the tree that is in the middle of the garden, nor shall you touch it, or you shall die.'" But the serpent said to the woman, "You will not die; for God knows that when you eat of it your eyes will be opened, and you will be like God, knowing good and evil." So when the woman saw that the tree was good for food, and that it was a delight to the eyes, and that the tree was to be desired to make one wise, she took of its fruit and ate; and she also gave some to her husband, who was with her, and he ate.

Temptation of Jesus in the Wilderness (Luke 4:1–13)

Jesus, full of the Holy Spirit, returned from the Jordan and was led by the Spirit in the wilderness, where for forty days he was tempted by the devil. He ate nothing at all during those days, and when they were over, he was famished. The devil said to him, "If you are the Son of God command this stone to become a loaf of bread." Jesus answered him, "It is written, 'One does not live by bread alone.'"

Then the devil led him up and showed him in an instant all the kingdoms of the world. And the devil said to him, "To you I will give their glory and all this authority; for it has been given over to me, and I give it to anyone I please. If you, then, will worship me, it will all be yours." Jesus answered him, "It is written, 'Worship the Lord your God, and serve only him.'"

Then the devil took him to Jerusalem, and placed him on the pinnacle of the temple, saying to him, "If you are the Son of God, throw yourself down from here, for it is written, 'He will command his angels concerning you, to protect you,' and 'On their hands they will bear you up, so that you will not dash your foot against a stone.'"

Jesus answered him, "It is said, 'Do not put the Lord your God to the test.'"

When the devil had finished every test, he departed from him until an opportune time.

Temptations Are Sure to Come (Luke 17:1–3)

Jesus said to his disciples, "Occasions for stumbling are bound to come, but woe to anyone by whom they come! It would be better for you if a millstone were hung around your neck and you were thrown into the sea than for you to cause one of these little ones to stumble. Be on your guard!"

Lead Us Not into Temptation (Matthew 6:13)

And do not bring us to the time of trial, but rescue us from the evil one.

Discussion Questions

Invite participants to take a look at how the two texts—the film Quiz Show *and the Bible—inform us, as people of faith, about the meaning of temptation in the life of a Christian.*

1. What are things commonly considered "temptations" (greed, lying, gossip, cheating, laziness, overwork, disloyalty, etc.)?
2. How would you describe your personal temptations? In what ways does your faith provide you with the strength to cope with temptation?
3. In what ways are we as individuals and as a country giving in to the temptation of selfishness by "borrowing" from those less fortunate than ourselves? From our children's futures?
4. Relate one of your own experiences to the passage from 1 Corinthians at the beginning of this chapter. What ways has God provided for you to "stand up" against a temptation you face?
5. Compare the temptations confronting Mark Van Doren with those faced by one of these figures from Scripture: Adam and Eve, Job, Jesus, Judas, or biblical characters of your own choosing. How are their temptations similar? How are they different?

Extension Activity

Invite group members to write a brief description of how the following "temptations" function in their own lives:

- ingratitude
- anxiety and worry
- self-criticism
- bending the rules
- overestimating appropriate influence over others and your life
- inability to let go
- lack of personal expression—keeping things bottled up; not sharing the best part of yourself
- putting yourself first/never putting yourself first

CHAPTER 5

Disappointment: How Do We Cope When Others Break Our Hearts?

The Music Box

ARTISAN ENTERTAINMENT, 1990, WITH JESSICA LANGE, ARMIN MUELLER-STAHL. DIRECTED BY CONSTANTIN COSTA-GAVRAS. RATED R FOR REFERENCES TO HOLOCAUST ATROCITIES.

Blessed is the man who expects nothing, for he shall never be disappointed . . .
    –Alexander Pope, 1725

"Could you not wait for me for one hour?"
    –Jesus to the sleeping disciples outside of the Garden of Gethsemane

Tips for Using This Movie

The Music Box addresses the theme of disappointment head-on. Of course, none of us is insulated from disappointment—with other people, with ourselves, with life. Disappointment with the actions of God—and God's disappointment with us—is also a universal theme within Scripture.

This intense and haunting film provides a powerful introduction to discussion of this topic by telling a story about a family and the deep bonds that bind them together, as well as the powerful force that threatens to sever their connection completely. It leaves the question hanging in the air for all to consider: After our hearts are broken and those we love have failed us—what then? There are a few graphic images in this film, but those appear only in still photographs and are quite brief. They are absolutely essential in the context of the movie, but viewers who might find them too strong can avert their eyes, since it is clear when they are coming.

If you are searching for more information on this film, be advised that there is also a 1938 Laurel and Hardy movie by the same name.

Background

Provide the background information that group members will need to follow the excerpts and put them into perspective by reading aloud—or adapting—this brief synopsis.

Against a passionate background of gypsy violins, Hungarian dancing, and the River Danube flowing red with the blood of martyrs, *The Music Box* tells the story of the intense love between a father and his daughter.

Ann Talbot (Jessica Lange) is a second-generation Hungarian; a divorced mother of a ten-year-old child; and an aggressive, respected attorney. Her father, Michael Laslo, came to the United States from Hungary thirty-seven years ago, following World War II. In Hungary he had been a farmer and later a soldier. Now his wife has died, his children are grown, he is retired from his job as a mill worker, and he is very close to his daughter and his grandson. He is an exemplary father and grandfather, affectionate, warm, and caring.

One day the family learns that the government is bringing startling and horrifying charges against Laslo, asserting that he was part of a select group of Hungarian Nazis who continued to persecute Jews even after the war had ended. They say his real name is "Mishka" and that he ordered and participated in dozens of brutal executions and other war crimes. Laslo insists that the charges are not only a case of mistaken identity, but also revenge from Hungary's Communist government.

Michael's daughter Ann rallies in passionate defense of her beloved father, serving as his attorney so that she can personally dispel the allegations and clear his name. As the trial progresses, Ann receives a packet of anonymous documents from Hungary, and she goes to Budapest to follow up on this information and to interview a key witness. Not until she returns to the United States does she discover the truth about her father—from a music box.

Reflection: It's Not Fair

Read this selection to the group. Or, you may wish to use this reflection as a springboard to writing a reflection of your own to share.

"But that's not fair!" was the rallying cry of my adolescent years. Not only did I get better grades than my younger brother Gordy, I seldom gave my parents any cause for worry. Yet he had no curfew, got to have a motorcycle at age sixteen, and never had to battle as I did for the many privileges he received. "But that's not fair!" I protested to my parents again and again.

Later, the experience of seeing my own daughters disappointed— often for reasons beyond their control—evoked the same reaction from me: "That is so unfair." Similarly, I seldom read a newspaper account of an exemplary human being forced to suffer through a horrible illness without mentally invoking my fairness litany.

Gradually, my naive belief that the world operates by clear standards of cause and effect or by a consistent standard of justice was eroded. I remember when I opened Scott Peck's landmark book, *A Road Less Traveled*, and read the first line: "Life is difficult."[6] Such a simple statement, and yet a deep confirmation of my own instincts. Okay, I thought, now I get it. But still, the wishful thinking remains . . .

Disappointment is predicated on the notion that our own standards and beliefs about the world are universal. It results from the misguided notion that our own worldview, God-view, and self-view prevail. Of course, they don't always, and the more attached we are to the ideas, people, and dreams we hold dear, the more it hurts when these things prove false. Yet we can also be pleasantly surprised when things are actually far better than we had imagined them to be.

Disappointment can set off a process of grieving for lost opportunities and dreams, of regret that we allowed ourselves to love so deeply and care so much, and of embarrassment that we were so completely taken in and misled. We can actively try to combat these feelings, rationalize them, suffer over them, or be resigned to them.

Perhaps disappointment is most bitter when we don't live up to our own expectations. It is especially difficult for those of us who somehow received the message at an early age that we had special abilities and people had great hopes for us. In my high school graduating class, I was voted "most likely to succeed"—and those words have come back to haunt me on a regular basis. We all ask ourselves if we are "succeeding," using our God-given gifts as best we can, or if we have compromised our talents.

Life itself has the capacity to disappoint us with cruel surprises. Nowhere is this more evident than in the biblical story of Job. Job undergoes a series of disappointing and horrifying losses before he asks God directly why all of these things are happening to him. God's response is to pull rank, reminding Job of God's role as Creator and Job's status as one of God's creatures. God lets Job know that some questions will simply not be answered in this lifetime.

We only seem to question God's goodness during difficult times. At the end of the movie *Awakenings*, the mother of a handicapped child remembers that when her child was born, so perfect and healthy, she never asked God "Why?" But ever since the child became ill, the question is always on her lips.

How would our lives be different if we, too, not only asked God "why" at times of aching disappointment, but also at times of abundant blessings?

Scenes to Use for a One-Hour Class
Set VCR to zero at "Carolco."

1. (9 min.) Ann dancing with her father to Hungarian music; credits; lawyers discussing cases; charges brought against Ann's father. End after Ann says, "Nobody's going to take away your citizenship, Papa."

     VCR—00:00 to 9:00   DVD—Scene 1
2. (25 min.) American phase of trial is over; witnesses are being examined in Budapest. Ann visits the house of the woman she

believes has a connection to the case; the woman gives her a pawnshop ticket to redeem when she gets home. Ann returns to America and goes to the pawnshop and, from a music box, learns the truth. She has a conversation with her father and writes a letter. End after she folds the letter for mailing.

VCR—1:35:00 to 2:00:00   DVD—Scene 21

Total running time: 34 minutes

Film, Faith, and Scripture

God's Disappointment with Adam and Eve (Genesis 3:11–12)

[God said to Adam:] "Who told you that you were naked? Have you eaten from the tree of which I commanded you not to eat?" The man said, "The woman whom you gave to be with me, she gave me fruit from the tree, and I ate."

God's Disappointment with Humankind (Genesis 6:5–6)

The Lord saw that the wickedness of humankind was great in the earth, and that every inclination of the thoughts of their hearts was only evil continually. And the Lord was sorry that he had made humankind on the earth and it grieved him to his heart.

Jesus Is Disappointed with His Disciples in the Garden of Gethsemane (Mark 14:34–41)

And he said to them, "I am deeply grieved, even to death; remain here, and keep awake. . . ." He came and found them sleeping, and he said to Peter, "Simon, are you asleep? Could you not keep awake one hour? Keep awake and pray that you may not come into the time of trial; the spirit indeed is willing, but the flesh is weak." And again he went away and prayed, saying the same words. And once more he came and found them sleeping, for their eyes were very heavy; and he did not know what to say to them. He came a third time and said to them, "Are you still sleeping and taking your rest? Enough! The hour has come . . . ."

Discussion Questions

Invite participants to look at how the two texts—The Music Box and the Bible—inform us, as people of faith, about the experience of disappointment and the ways God sustains us—and transforms us during these times.

1. How did Ann Talbot deal with her deep sense of disappointment and betrayal at the end of the film? Do you think she made the right choice?

2. Recall a specific time in your life when someone disappointed you in an important way. How did you respond to the disappointment? To what degree is the intensity of that experience still with you? How did Jesus respond to disappointment? How did Ann?

3. What are some common methods of dealing with disappointment? (You might discuss denial, rationalization, anger, sadness, resignation, guilt, revenge, change in behavior, or forgiveness.)

4. Respond to this rabbinic maxim: "May we cease to be a cause of suffering to one another." What is one specific thing you could do in your own life to avoid disappointing another person? Would there be a cost to you if you followed such a strategy?

5. What do the three stories from Scripture in this chapter have in common? What are the things that seem to most disappoint God?

6. In what ways does God seem to respond to disappointment? Give examples from Scripture.

7. What are things you do each day that may disappoint God? Which of your actions do you think please God?

8. What do you think the music box symbolizes?

Extension Activity

Invite members of the group to bring an object with them to the next meeting that is an icon of a central event in their lives. Invite them either to write about the object or be prepared to talk about what it means to them.

CHAPTER 6

Envy: Why Is Jealousy a Sin?

Amadeus

ORION PICTURES, 1984, WITH TOM HULCE, F. MURRAY ABRAHAM.
DIRECTED BY MILOS FORMAN; WINNER OF EIGHT ACADEMY
AWARDS, INCLUDING BEST PICTURE, BEST ACTOR (ABRAHAM), BEST
DIRECTOR. RATED PG.

God writes my music.
   –Johann Sebastian Bach

Now there are varieties of gifts, but the same Spirit, . . . and
there are varieties of activities, but it is the same God who
activates all of them in everyone.
   –1 Corinthians 12:4, 6

You shall not covet . . .
   –Exodus 20:17

Tips for Using This Movie

This is a "big" movie in every sense: in the scope and historical significance of the material, in the complicated plot that shifts back and
forth from past to present, in the stature and forcefulness of the main

characters, and in the powerful musical score that is alternately lyrical and thunderous.

The film clips selected make this formidable movie manageable for a one-hour class. Three of the four scenes are monologues on one character's jealousy of the other, and the blame he places on God for his misfortune. The other scene is a humorous yet shattering account of the first time the two characters meet. And then, of course, there is Mozart's music . . .

Be sure to present the setting of the story, drawn from the background notes, before you show the clips. However, each clip selected can stand on its own as an individual statement about the theme of envy, so you may want to briefly discuss each scene after seeing it, and then move to the questions suggested at the end.

If time permits, at the end of the discussion you may want to play a few minutes of the movie's ending: scenes from Mozart's burial in a pauper's grave accompanied by excerpts from his *Requiem,* the score he wrote for his own funeral.

Background

To provide a context for the excerpts and to help participants follow the movie line, read this background information to the group.

The threatening, ominous, and discordant musical sting that begins *Amadeus* (taken from the opera *Don Giovanni*) tells us immediately that all is not well.

In eighteenth-century Vienna, where the story takes place, human struggles are everywhere, from the efforts of the lower classes to physically survive to the lofty tiffs and competitions among the court musicians who are part of Emperor Joseph II's entourage. Nowhere is the struggle more intense than in the battle of the former child prodigy Wolfgang Amadeus Mozart to get his music performed and accepted, and in the internal struggle of his competitor, court composer Antonio Salieri, to come to terms with Mozart's genius.

Described by author and screenwriter Peter Schaffer as "a fantasia based on fact," this movie presents challenging questions: Why does God bestow genius on seeming fools? What happens when art becomes competition? How do you make peace with the gifts you are given, instead of letting envy of others destroy your soul?

Most of the film is recounted from the perspective of Salieri as an old man, mentally ill, delusional, yet remarkably honest and perceptive in his memories. The film encompasses not only Salieri's flashbacks, but also a chronology of critical events in the life of Mozart.

We see Mozart as a child, taught music by his father and pushed mercilessly to perform as a pianist and violinist in the concert halls of Europe. An amazing prodigy, he wrote his first symphony at nine, his first opera at twelve. Much of the movie centers on Mozart's later struggles to get his operas performed (he wrote forty) amidst the politics and fickle preferences of the emperor and his court.

In a sense, this is Salieri's story, because his consuming jealousy drives the plot. Salieri bargains with God that if only God will grant him unparalleled talent, he will use it for the sole purpose of divine praise. However, Mozart's genius convinces Salieri that God has not acquiesced to the deal.

Salieri embodies an especially painful form of jealousy. He has enough talent to hear (as many others do not) Mozart's brilliance. (Indeed, "Amadeus" means "loved by God.") Salieri laments that all that God has given him is "the ability to recognize the incarnation." From that point on, Salieri sets out to destroy "the creature" (as he calls Mozart) by exploiting Mozart's feelings for his father.

Herr Mozart has disapproved of the direction of his son's career and frowns on his bohemian lifestyle, drinking, and lack of discipline. After Herr Mozart's sudden death, Mozart, haunted by his father's memory, and driven to compose his great opera, *Don Giovanni,* works himself to his own death. Along the way, he is prodded and tricked by Salieri, whose sole purpose for existence has become the destruction of his rival.

One of the most powerful aspects of this film is the score, Mozart's music, arranged and conducted by Neville Marriner. At the end, as Mozart is buried in a pauper's grave, we hear segments from his last composition and one of his most glorious works, his own *Requiem.*

Reflection: Composing Our Lives

Read this selection to the group. Or, you may wish to use this reflection as a springboard to writing a reflection of your own to share with the group.

Do not conspire in your own diminishment.[7]
   –Parker Palmer

How petty the circumstances that can breed jealousy, that can be called back in a heartbeat, decades later. In retrospect, often we can't believe that the envy we once felt brought us such pain.

When I was in high school in the 1960s, more than anything I wanted to be a cheerleader. Although I tried for four years, I never was one of the lucky girls selected. How I envied the cheerleader lifestyle—the popularity that came with the job, the girls' camaraderie and fun in front of the crowd at sporting events, the jaunty uniforms, the fact that one of them was always chosen homecoming queen, the power that cheerleaders wielded in the school. I would sit in the bleachers at basketball games and wonder why I wasn't born prettier, why my friends always seemed to be in the "second tier" of popularity, why being a nerdy debater was the only role that brought me success.

I see now how much this aching jealousy and envy hurt me, not only by inflicting emotional pain, but also by blinding me to my own considerable gifts and blessings, or at least shamefully minimizing them in my own mind.

How silly all of this seems now. How embarrassing that this still sticks in my mind—it was high school, for goodness sake! How grateful I am that I was forced to aspire to more than what I wanted then so desperately. Yet, at the time, I was blinded by the flashing red and gold pom-poms that always eluded me. And the pain of it can still be called up in a moment.

Like all of us, I've had successful moments in my life, but when they arrive, I tend to minimize them and wish I'd done even better. These words from writer Bill Holm always strike a chord with me: "Though not so good a musician as to have made a genuine living from it, I was good enough to know the precise deficiencies of every performance I ever gave."[8]

What we refer to as jealousy and envy is called "coveting" in Scripture. One of the Ten Commandments warns us not to "covet" those things belonging to our neighbor (Exodus 20:17). The language in Genesis specifies our neighbor's wife, slaves, ox, and donkey as off limits, yet it's easy to translate these terms into contemporary equivalents. Each of us could make our own list of what it is we so desperately want and don't have.

Following the disobedience of Adam and Eve, one of the first "sins" that appears in Genesis is that of jealousy, as Cain murders his brother Abel because God found Abel's offering more pleasing. From that point on, jealousy makes regular appearances in Scripture.

Yet God seems to understand that our hearts are filled with yearnings and longings that are not exactly envy or jealousy, but more of an aching emptiness. The psalmist says, "As a deer longs for flowing streams, so my soul longs for you, O God" (Psalm 42:1). The psalmist is confident that God understands this yearning: "O Lord, all my longing is known to you; my sighing is not hidden from you" (Psalm 38:9).

While we may yearn to dwell in inner peace, to experience a closer relationship with God, or simply to have the empty space in our hearts filled, jealousy and envy are more specific and less benign. For one thing, they call our relationship with God into question. It's hard not to wonder what God had in mind passing out the gifts. Scripture attests that all are given different gifts, but sometimes that isn't much consolation if it seems like we received more challenges than talent, more problems than bounty. Part of our life's work is coming to terms with our portion and learning to use it with confidence and joy.

One way of approaching the reality of jealousy in human life may be to change our understanding of success. Mary Catherine Bateson talks about two models for imaging success, as a ladder or as a patchwork quilt. She says that a linear concept of success, like climbing the corporate ladder, is a popular model in our culture, especially for males. But this model can result in jealousy and resentment when people get stuck—especially when they're trying their hardest to climb higher.

However, Bateson's other model of successful achievement, the patchwork quilt, assembles the aspects of a person's life like pieces of a quilt, with each patch representing an accomplishment, a stage of life, or even a tragedy that's been lived through. This image recognizes the necessity of improvisation, acknowledges that detours and sidetracks often pull us off our original path, and respects the fact that important aspects of human life don't fit into a linear pattern.

Many of us have to reinvent ourselves again and again, depending on our careers, lifestyles, and luck. Bateson asserts, "It is time now to explore the creative potential of interrupted and conflicted lives . . .

and at what point does desperate improvisation become significant achievement?"[9]

It is an achievement indeed when we can view our own lives as a composition we are in the process of creating, both from the raw material life has handed us and the love that God gives us to guide our hands and our hearts.

Scenes to Use for a One-Hour Class
Set at zero at "HBO Video" for VCR.

1. (8 min.) Mozart has died and former court composer Salieri is confined to an asylum in Vienna. A priest arrives to hear his confession. Salieri remembers his earlier life and curses Mozart. End after Salieri says: "Until he came . . ."
   VCR—5:35 to 13:45   DVD—begin at Scene 1
2. (8 min.) Salieri remembers the day Mozart first arrived at court. Mozart plays a march of welcome Salieri has written in his honor and humiliates him. Salieri's soliloquy on talent. End after Salieri says, ". . . then deny me the talent."
   VCR—29:00 to 37:00   DVD—begin at Scene 8
3. (6 min.) Scene of deer in the forest opens this segment. The Emperor passes on Salieri in favor of Mozart to tutor his niece. Salieri remembers the day that Mrs. Mozart comes to him for help, and shows him her husband's musical scores. End after Salieri says, "I will ruin your incarnation."
   VCR—51:00 to 57:00   DVD—begin at Scene 12
4. (optional) (4 min.) (can be used with VCR; difficult to locate on DVD) Portions of Mozart's Requiem played during his pauper's burial. End as Mozart's casket lay in the ground.
   VCR—2:28:00 to 2:32:00

Running time: 23 minutes (excluding segment 4 on VCR; otherwise, add 4 min.)

Film, Faith, and Scripture

Explore with your group the connections between film, faith, and Scripture by examining what the Bible says to us about the ways

envy affects our relationships with God, other people, and our-
selves. You may read the scripture passages from your book, or ask
participants to look them up and read them to the group.

Cain's Jealousy of Abel (Genesis 4:3–8)

In the course of time Cain brought to the Lord an offering of the fruit
of the ground, and Abel for his part brought of the firstlings of his
flock, their fat portions. And the Lord had regard for Abel and his
offering, but for Cain and his offering he had no regard.

So Cain was very angry, and his countenance fell. The Lord said
to Cain, "Why are you angry and why has your countenance fallen?
If you do well, will you not be accepted? And if you do not do well,
sin is lurking at your door; its desire is for you, but you must master
it . . . ." And when they were in the field, Cain rose up against this
brother Abel, and killed him.

The Patriarchs Are Jealous of Joseph (Acts 7:9–10)

The patriarchs, jealous of Joseph, sold him into Egypt; but God was
with him, and rescued him from all his afflictions, and enabled him to
win favor and show wisdom when he stood before Pharaoh . . . .

Jealousy and Cravings Lead to Conflict (James 4:1–3)

Those conflicts and disputes among you, where do they come from?
Do they not come from your cravings that are at war within you? You
want something and do not have it; so you commit murder. And you
covet something and cannot obtain it; so you engage in disputes and
conflicts. You do not have, because you do not ask. You ask and do not
receive, because you ask wrongly, in order to spend what you get on
your pleasures.

Different Gifts (1 Corinthians 2:12)

Now we have received not the spirit of the world, but the Spirit that
is from God, so that we may understand the gifts bestowed on us
by God.

God's Gifts Vary (1 Corinthians 7:7)

Each has a particular gift from God, one having one kind and another a different kind.

Jesus Warns the Disciples about Competition (Luke 13:30)

"Indeed some are last who will be fist, and some are first who will be last."

Discussion Questions

Invite participants to take a look at how the two texts—the film Amadeus *and the Bible—inform us, as people of faith, about the ways that jealousy and envy impede our relationship with God and one another, and diminish our God-given talents.*

1. Which of Salieri's statements could you most identify with? Why? Can you relate them in any way to your own experience?
2. Who is someone in public life that you are envious of? Why? What types of people do you tend to be jealous of?
3. What do you covet now? Has jealousy ever threatened to consume you?
   - What or who were you jealous of?
   - How did the jealousy damage you at the time?
   - How did the situation resolve itself? What, if anything, did you learn from this experience?
4. What keeps you desiring the gifts of others rather than celebrating the ones you yourself have received? Salieri was a highly gifted musician in his own right. What prevented him from glorifying God through his own craft and impelled him to focus on the gifts of Mozart?
5. What are some abilities that you have that you minimize or seldom acknowledge? Why do you do this? In what ways do you "conspire in your own diminishment" at your job? In your relationships? In other ways?
6. Describe a moment when you have felt: "This is the reason why I was born; this is what God put me here to do." (A good prayer: "God, help me live up to my calling.")

7. Spend a few minutes thinking about the following statement: "Focus more on who you are, and less on who you aren't." What insights has this experience brought you?

Extension Activity

Respond in writing or in a small group to the following questions:

- What do you think is one of the greatest talents that God has bestowed on you?
- What makes you feel that this is a divine gift?
- How have you used this gift?
- How could you use it more fully? More joyfully?
- What keeps you from using it to its fullest extent?

CHAPTER 7

Suffering: How Do We Understand the Problem of Pain?

Shadowlands

SAVOY PICTURES, 1993, WITH ANTHONY HOPKINS, DEBRA WINGER. DIRECTED BY RICHARD ATTENBOROUGH; BRITISH ACADEMY AWARD FOR BEST ACTOR. RATED PG.

Deep, unspeakable suffering may well be called a baptism, a regeneration into a new state.
    –George Eliot

He considered abuse suffered for Christ to be greater wealth than the treasures of Egypt, for he was looking ahead to the reward.
    –Hebrews 11:26

Tips for Using This Movie

This is a tremendous movie for discussing a key issue in virtually every religion: the meaning of suffering. It also provides insight into an important figure in Anglicanism: novelist and theologian C. S. Lewis. Strongly urge people to watch the entire movie eventually, because each scene presents its own riches. However, the excerpts selected here do a good job of presenting the key aspects of the story and theme.

The conclusion of *Shadowlands* is overwhelming in the emotional reaction it evokes; it will touch the audience members at their core. Following the clips—which should be shown in sequence with only the transitional explanations interrupting them—allow a period of silence before discussion commences—and bring tissues to distribute! This heartbreaking yet lovely film has a compelling message for all of us who suffer because we take the risk to love. It is not to be missed.

Background

To provide a context for the excerpts and to help participants follow the movie line, read this background information to the group.

When he was nine years old, C. S. Lewis's mother died. The pain of losing her was so intense for the young boy that from that point on, he shut down his emotions, building a thick wall between himself and the world so as not to be hurt again.

The story begins in the 1950s. Lewis is a professor at Oxford, immersing himself in the life of the mind. It is a gentleman's life, filled with reading, conversation, and debates about theology with other professors over sherry and cigars. At the same time, Lewis, living with his bachelor brother and unacquainted with any little ones, is writing strangely magical books for children. His books make him much sought after as a speaker who talks about Christianity in terms everyone can understand.

In his lectures and speeches, Lewis teaches that the most intense joy possible is desire—the quest for what you want but don't have. He proclaims that this is far superior to actually getting what you desire, which is certain to be disappointing. So to Lewis, the potential and promise of the rosebud is far more beautiful than the fully opened flower, which will soon fade and disintegrate. Perhaps, he implies, it's even safer to stay away from roses altogether.

His beliefs about God have a similar theme. Lewis teaches that God molds us and makes us stronger by sending us suffering and pain. He is fond of saying, "God whispers to us in our pleasures, speaks in our conscience, but shouts in our pain. It is his megaphone to rouse a deaf world."

These theories work well for Lewis, since he has put a wall around his life that keeps out all but superficial connections with the people who could hurt him, and he lives a life of the head and not the heart. A safe life—or so he thinks.

When Lewis is in his late forties, he meets Joy Gresham, a divorced Jewish-American poet who visits Oxford and seeks Lewis out because she admires his work. Though he fights valiantly against it, Lewis falls deeply in love with Joy. This is the first time that his wall has cracked, the first time he has allowed himself to love since his mother died.

A short time after their intense and passionate relationship begins, Joy becomes ill, diagnosed with an aggressive form of bone cancer. Although the disease goes into remission, it soon returns worse than ever. It becomes clear that she will not recover.

On one of her better days, Joy and "Jack" (as Lewis is called) go on a picnic in the English countryside, awash with the colors, sounds, and fresh smells of spring. Lewis tells Joy that he knows now that possessing something is infinitely better than just wanting it—that a single moment of true, full happiness is "enough" for him, far better than constantly anticipating what might be around the next corner. Joy reminds him that moments end and life changes, and that she is going to die—probably soon. Lewis, distraught, says that her death will devastate him but that he will "manage." She tells him he can do better than that if he sees life in a different way. She reminds him, "The happiness now is part of the pain then. That's the deal."

Following Joy's death, Lewis is inconsolable. As he reflects on what has happened, he wonders if it was worth it to love so intensely, only to have his heart torn apart. For the first time in his life, intellect doesn't help. It is through his return to teaching and in his continuing care for Joy's young son, Joseph, who now lives with him, that his healing begins.

Reflection: The Deal

Read this selection to the group. Or, you may wish to use this reflection as a springboard to writing a reflection of your own to share with the group.

In her autobiography *Black Ice,* Lorene Carey talks about her high school years in the 1970s as the first student of color at an exclusive New England boarding school. Her time there was difficult and painful as she came to terms with her less-than-privileged economic background and her status as a minority in a rich, white world.

Though she is often guarded, suspicious, and self-critical, she receives a new insight at her graduation ceremony. As she goes forward with another student named Tom to claim the awards they're being given, she realizes that at St. Paul's she'd rejected two acts of kindness—the headmaster's gift of plane tickets to fly home when her mother was sick and Tom's offer of friendship. She concludes: "I had not loved enough. I'd been busy, busy, so busy preparing for life, while life floated by me, quiet and swift as a regatta."[10] On a deep level, she acknowledges that there would be no more chances for her to correct the situation, at least at school. Her time there was up.

This is the realization that many of us reach when something is over—at a parting, a death, even at the end of the year. I have not loved enough. I have not loved often enough. I have not given people a chance. I have not engaged. I have remained aloof, busy, preoccupied, until something changes and then these people and these circumstances—these days—seem heartbreakingly precious in hindsight.

So often it seems that loving enough—friends, colleagues, even family members—costs us something. It costs effort and energy, and it brings the inevitable burdens and complexities of engaging with other human beings. It is as if affirming and supporting people, complimenting them, telling them you care about them, diminishes a store of finite resources within us, and we choose not to pay the price at the moment. The good news is that these internal resources are not finite, but renewable, often through the very actions that we fear will diminish them.

If we love—other people, our jobs, our healthy bodies, our lives as they are—we open ourselves up to loss and suffering. At the end of *Shadowlands,* Lewis says, "Twice in my life I've been given the choice. As a boy, I chose safety. As a man, I chose suffering." In his case, as in ours, a decision to love is simultaneously a decision to allow suffering into our lives. In novelist John Updike's words, this is "the vulnerability to which love dooms us all."

Of course, playing by the rules doesn't insulate us from suffering and pain. Biblical figures from Job to Jesus have lamented this reality.

A basic Christian belief is that the death of Jesus on the cross acknowledges the suffering inherent in the human condition and calls us beyond the pain to resurrection and renewal. However, we can also learn about God's attitude towards human suffering when we look at the actions and responses of Jesus. Philip Yancey writes that Jesus always responds to the plight of the suffering with compassion and empathy, never telling those in pain to "buck up." He says, "The pattern of Jesus' responses should convince us that God is not a God who enjoys seeing us suffer. I doubt that Jesus' disciples tormented themselves with questions like 'Does God care?' They had visible evidence of his concern every day; they simply looked at Jesus' face."[11]

Combating the loneliness that so often accompanies pain is a formidable challenge. In the film, a student suggests to Lewis, "We read to know we're not alone." Later, after he has been through the experience of losing Joy, Lewis amends the phrase, telling the student that perhaps "we love to know we're not alone."

Ultimately, Lewis admits he has no answer to the question of whether to choose safety or love "other than the life I've lived." Just as, in some mysterious way only God knows, pain and love are inextricably linked: "That's the deal."

Excerpts to Use for a One-Hour Class
Set VCR to zero at "Savoy Pictures."

1. (4 min.) Lewis and his brother are in a restaurant waiting to meet Joy Gresham, an American writer who admires his work. Joy arrives; they converse. Lewis shows Joy a bit of Oxford. End after Joy says, "New, heh?" and Lewis replies, "1733."
   VCR—13:20 to 16:44   DVD—begin at Scene 3.
2. (9 min.) Joy and Jack arrive at a hotel in the country. They go on a picnic and talk about the fact that Joy feels she will die soon. End after the kiss in the rain.
   VCR—1:39:00 to 1:48:00   DVD—begin at Scene 19
3. (11 min.) Joy's funeral. Jack and Warnie reflect on life. Jack returns to teaching and later has a conversation with Joy's son, Joseph. Go to end of film.
   VCR—1:57:00 to end   DVD—begin at Scene 22
Total running time: 24 minutes

Film, Faith, and Scripture

Explore with your group the connections between film, faith, and Scripture by examining what the Bible says to us about the meaning of human suffering. You may read the scripture passages from this book, or ask participants to look them up and read them to the group.

The Suffering Servant (Isaiah 53:3, 5)

He was despised and rejected by others; a man of suffering and acquainted with infirmity; and as one from whom others hide their faces he was despised, and we held him of no account. . . . But he was wounded for our transgressions, crushed for our iniquities; upon him was the punishment that made us whole, and by his bruises we are healed.

Suffering Transcends Boundaries (1 Corinthians 12:26)

If one member suffers, all suffer together with it; if one member is honored, all rejoice together with it.

Privileges (Philippians 1:29)

For he has graciously granted you not only the privilege of believing in Christ, but of suffering for him as well.

God Reminds Job Who Created the World (excerpts from Job 38: 1, 4–5, 12)

Then the Lord answered Job out of the whirlwind . . . "Where were you when I laid the foundation of the earth? Tell me, if you have understanding. Who determined its measurements—surely you know! . . . Have you commanded the morning since your days began, and caused the dawn to know its place?"

Discussion Questions

1. Describe a point in your life when have you chosen "safety" over potential suffering. What have been the results of this choice? What did you gain by avoiding suffering? What did you lose by avoiding it?

2. Do you think Joy is right when she asserts that the "deal" is that happiness in our lives is usually followed by pain (or vice versa)? A collect in The Book of Common Prayer (Service of Compline) calls us to "shield the joyous." What must they be "shielded" from?

3. A student tells Lewis: "We read to know we're not alone." What is a particular story or passage from Scripture that makes you feel less alone? How did the passage help you put your suffering into context? What did you learn about suffering?

4. In his famous "I Have a Dream" speech, the Reverend Martin Luther King Jr. asserted that "unearned suffering is redemptive." What do you think this means? In what ways was Lewis redeemed by his unearned suffering? What about Joy? What about Jesus? How about you?

5. What answer does God give Job about the meaning and unfairness of suffering? Is it a comforting response or a troubling one?

Extension Activities

1. Where have you "not loved enough"—today? This week? This year? Has this failure to love caused you to suffer in any way? Write a short reflection on these questions or share your response in a small group.

2. Watch the movie The Shawshank Redemption and consider how the main character comes to terms with the difficulties in his life.

CHAPTER 8

Forgiveness: How Do We Give and Accept Forgiveness?

Smoke Signals

MIRIMAX PICTURES, 1998, WITH ADAM BEACH, ERIN ADAMS, TANTOO CARDINAL. DIRECTED BY CHRIS EYRE; WINNER OF AUDIENCE AWARD AND FILMMAKER'S TROPHY AT SUNDANCE FILM FESTIVAL. RATED PG-13.

To forgive wrongs darker than death or night . . .
To love and bear; to hope till Hope creates
From its own wreck the thing it contemplates . . .
Good, great and joyous, beautiful and free.
    –Percy Bysshe Shelley, *Prometheus Unbound*, 570

And forgive us our debts, as we also have forgiven our debtors.
    –Matthew 6:12

Tips for Using This Movie

The ending of *Smoke Signals* contains one of the most poetic and insightful statements about the nature of forgiveness ever put on film, and this alone makes the movie worth seeing. However, it has much more to recommend it. It is a story of the complex dynamics that evolve within a family and how even anger, alcoholism, and hurt cannot defeat love. All of this is presented in a context that is new to most non–Native American viewers: daily life on a contemporary Indian reservation. The clips selected give a taste of the sadness, humor, and lyricism of the film, but most viewers will eventually want to watch the film in its entirety.

Smoke Signals forces viewers to reach deep down into their psyches to explore their own personal experiences of forgiveness. After the last clip—which includes the end of the movie—ask participants to be silent for a moment. Then play the closing monologue a second time. Its impact will be even greater, especially for those who have had troubled relationships with their own fathers. Structure discussion around the two aspects of forgiveness: giving and receiving.

The "Reflection" enlarges the topic of forgiveness from the personal realm of the movie to larger political and social arenas.

Background

To provide a context for the excerpts and to help participants follow the movie line, read this background information to the group.

"It's a beautiful day on the reservation this morning. It's a good day to be indigenous!" proclaims the announcer on KREZ radio, "the official voice of the Coer d'Alene people."

Based on screenwriter Sherman Alexie's book, *The Lone Ranger and Tonto Fistfight in Heaven*, this movie is part drama and part comedy. It is billed as the first feature film written, directed, produced, and acted by Native Americans.

The movie begins on the Fourth of July, 1976, on the Coer d'Alene reservation in Idaho at a party celebrating "white people's independence." As the evening grows late, a house fire erupts, killing two tribal members who are the parents of an infant. Baby Thomas is saved because he is thrown out a window ("flying," as Thomas says later) by a big, gruff man named Arnold Joseph, himself the father of a baby named Victor.

The movie fast-forwards nearly twenty years and we meet Thomas and Victor again as young men. Victor, tall, handsome, serious, is not completely recovered from the fact that his father, Arnold Joseph, deserted the family ten years earlier. Thomas—the baby thrown to safety in the fire—is a bespectacled, suit-wearing, dreamy boy who lives with his eccentric grandmother and prides himself on being a storyteller. Despite their differences, Thomas and Victor are friends.

Victor receives word that his father has died in Arizona, and he and Thomas make the long journey by bus and on foot to retrieve Arnold Joseph's truck and belongings. It is during this trip that Victor learns more about his father—not only about the demons he battled, but also about the deep and abiding love he had for his son.

At the end of the movie when Thomas asks Victor, "So why did your dad leave?" Victor, acknowledging the complexity of human motivation, replies, "He didn't mean to, Thomas." And Victor then sets about doing what he has to do to grieve his father's death and face the question of forgiveness. The film addresses the important questions of why we hurt the ones we love—and if we can or should be forgiven.

Smoke Signals begins with fire and flames and ends on a bridge over Spokane Falls, the waters below at once raging and cleansing. The closing monologue, adapted from a longer poem from the book *Ghost Radio,* is a breathtaking and haunting riff on the complexity of forgiveness.[12]

But *Smoke Signals* explores not only forgiveness between family members. It also explores the broader cultural and historical questions: How can a race of native people forgive generations of oppression by the American government? And how can young Indians forgive their parents and grandparents, who let it happen?

Reflection: For We Know Not What We Do

Read this selection to the group. Or, you may wish to use this reflection as a springboard to writing a reflection of your own to share with the group.

It's difficult to contemplate forgiveness when you're paralyzed with fear.

In the guarded, anxious, and fear-heightened climate in which Americans now live, forgiveness is probably the last thing on our minds. Since September 11, 2001, when the sense of invulnerability Americans had lived with for so long was shattered by attacks on the Twin Towers and the Pentagon, our sensibilities have been seared and our sense of national safety shattered. Each time we turn on a news broadcast, we're reminded again that our world, our country, and our neighborhoods are not safe.

Yet the scriptural mandate to forgive remains. We are exhorted not to pass judgment on our brothers and sisters (Romans 14:5) and to "forgive our brothers and sisters from our hearts" (Matthew 18:21). Jesus does not define our brothers and sisters. They are simply other human beings—maybe mistaken in their motives, negligent in their duty, or sinners in the most reprehensible and evil sense—but still God's children, still accountable to God.

So are we supposed to forgive terrorists? Murderers and rapists? Forgive those who stand in line for the privilege of destroying us and use religion as a weapon to drive planes into buildings? Forgive those who prey on innocent victims who happen to be at the wrong place at the wrong time?

In religious terms, forgiveness is not always simple. Jesus seems to say that forgiveness is, to some degree, dependent on an accompanying change in behavior. Similarly, The Book of Common Prayer says that "true repentance" must precede forgiveness, along with "amendment of life."[13] Forgiveness is not automatic. We don't dispense it smiling and unthinkingly; we don't chant the familiar litany: "Oh, that's okay"—"No problem"—"I'll get over it." People who abuse and mistreat children, alcoholics who refuse to confront the havoc their behavior wreaks in their families, those who engage in sexual misconduct that destroys trust and love are not helped by too-easy forgiveness with no accountability for their actions, especially when these destructive actions are repeated and intentional. Forgiving others is not sentimental niceness; it is serious business.

Of course, forgiveness is most difficult when an individual's actions are reprehensible by any existing moral code. How do we even begin to think in any clear way about people who seem beyond redemption and who have the capacity and the will to hurt us? How do we get by our fear and our wounds and see the child of God that lurks beneath?

The Reverend Cecil Murray has one suggestion. He is pastor of First African Methodist Episcopal Church in a troubled district in downtown Los Angeles. With seven thousand members, it's an active, socially conscious parish at the heart of its neighborhood. Murray was asked how he could deal with so many people who have failed by society's standards—either through criminal activity or by failing to achieve material success. He responded, "Because I know why they're not achieving. At a critical juncture in their life, they went that way and I went another way. Now why did I go that way? Somebody whispered something in my ear, something good, and somebody failed to whisper in his ear or her ear something good."[14]

Everyone—our own parents, our neighbors, even fanatical terrorists—has a story with twists and turns, lessons learned and rejected, possessions given and taken away, dreams fulfilled and deferred. Each of us can recall moments when powerful words, whispered or shouted, determined the course of our lives.

But it is not only a question of granting forgiveness, but of seeking it as well. What do we ourselves need to ask forgiveness for—from others? From God? In her book *In Search of Belief,* Joan Chittister says that the quintessential twentieth-century sin among the developed nations of the world is the sin of disregard. It is not thinking about the Third World and the hundreds who die there each day from starvation; it is feigning ignorance of those who work for pennies a day and support our low supermarket prices; it is turning our backs on requests for help because we have "compassion fatigue."

The sin of disregard is pretending not to notice the person in the office next to us who is clearly hurting; it is avoiding the newspaper article about a sweatshop in Korea because we can't do anything about it anyway; it is refusing to recycle because it's too much trouble. It's not so much conscious, premeditated evil, Chittister says, as it is "self-centered disregard for the rest of the human race, for the little people on whose shoulders we all stand, for the evil effects of our lives on the lives of others."[15]

Only God sees the intricacies of our hearts; only God understands why we ignore the needy; only God knows what causes people to blow up buildings full of people—or nail an innocent man to a cross. But with his last breath, Jesus utters the mysterious words that encompass it all: "Father, forgive them, for they do not know what they are doing."

Nor do we.

Film Clips to Use for a One-Hour Class
Set VCR to zero at "Miramax Films."

1. (11 min.) Credits. 1976: party on the reservation. Baby Thomas is saved by Arnold Joseph. Flash forward to 1998: traffic report

for KREZ; Thomas and Victor as teenagers and flashback to them as young boys. Arnold Joseph leaves the family; news of his death arrives; Thomas begs to accompany Victor. End after Victor says to Thomas: "You're funny."

> VCR—00:00 to 11:00   DVD—begin at Scene 2

2. (1 min.) Flashback: to the day Arnold Joseph left. End after Victor's mother says, "You feel that way, too, huh?"

> VCR—32:21 to 33:20   DVD—begin at Scene 10

3. (3 min.) In Phoenix, Victor talks with his dad's neighbor, Susie Song. Flashback to the basketball game with the Jesuits. End after Susie says, "He was a magician, you know."

> VCR—52:00 to 54:30   DVD—begin at Scene 15

4. (5 min.) Thomas and Victor return to the reservation; Victor scatters his father's ashes over Spokane Falls; monologue on forgiveness. Continue to the end of the movie.

> VCR—1:16:00 to end   DVD—begin at Scene 20

Total running time: 20 minutes

Film, Faith, and Scripture

Explore with your group the connections between film, faith, and Scripture by examining what the Bible says to us about forgiveness. You may read the scripture passages from your book, or ask participants to look them up and read them to the group.

The Parable of the Unforgiving Servant (Matthew 18:23–35)

"For this reason the kingdom of heaven may be compared to a king who wished to settle accounts with his slaves. When he began the reckoning, one who owed him ten thousand talents was brought to him; and, as he could not pay, his lord ordered him to be sold, together with his wife and children and all his possessions, and payment to be made. So the slave fell on his knees before him, saying, 'Have patience with me, and I will pay you everything.' And out of pity for him, the lord of that slave released him and forgave him the debt.

But that same slave, as he went out, came upon one of his fellow slaves who owed him a hundred denarii; and seizing him by the throat, he said, 'Pay what you owe.' Then his fellow slave fell down and pleaded with him, 'Have patience with me, and I will pay you.' But he refused; then he went and threw him into prison until he would pay the debt.

When his fellow slaves saw what had happened, they were greatly distressed, and they went and reported to their lord all that had taken place. Then his lord summoned him and said to him, 'You wicked slave! I forgave you all that debt because you pleaded with me. Should you not have had mercy on your fellow slave, as I had mercy on you?' And in anger his lord handed him over to be tortured until he would pay his entire debt. So my heavenly Father will also do to every one of you, if you do not forgive your brother or sister from your heart."

Jesus on the Cross (Luke 23:34)

Then Jesus said, "Father, forgive them; for they do not know what they are doing."

Discussion Questions

Invite participants to take a look at what the two texts—the film Smoke Signals *and the Bible—teach us about the ways that forgiveness is central to our faith.*

1. The last line of the movie asks, "If we forgive our fathers, what is left?" After we forgive someone who has hurt us deeply and repeatedly, what is left? What does the act of forgiveness force us to come to terms with about ourselves? How does forgiveness cleanse and transform us? What is left after Jesus forgives his tormenters?
2. From the excerpts you watched, do you think it would have been difficult for Arnold Joseph to seek—or accept—forgiveness? What things make it difficult for you to accept forgiveness—from another person? From God? How does the act of accepting forgiveness change us?
3. In the story of the unforgiving servant, why do you think the servant who was so generously forgiven refused to forgive the person who was indebted to him?

Unity Library and Archives

4. Being specific, explain how you commit "the sin of disregard." Who are some of the people whose sacrifices make your own lifestyle possible? Is thanking them a realistic option? Are there any ways in which personally or as a society we seek to make amends?

5. In our own lives or in our national life, are there times when forgiveness of others is not an option? Consider, as you ponder this question, the popular mantra: "What would Jesus do?"

Extension Activities

Respond to the following questions individually in writing or as part of a small group, sharing what you wish:

1. The powerful poem that ends the film begins with the question, "How do we forgive our fathers?" Who is someone from your own life that you most need to forgive and have not yet forgiven? What has prevented this?

2. What are some things you have said or done (or thought) that need forgiveness? Who do you need to ask forgiveness from— and why? What would you say?

An excellent poem to seek out on the topic of forgiving our fathers is "Late Poem to My Father," by Sharon Olds, in *The Gold Cell: Poems by Sharon Olds* (New York: Alfred A. Knopf), 1982.

CHAPTER 9

Gratitude: How Is Beauty a Gateway to Thankfulness?

American Beauty

DREAMWORKS, 1999, WITH KEVIN SPACEY, ANNETTE BENNING. DIRECTED BY SAM MENDES; ACADEMY AWARDS FOR BEST PICTURE, BEST ACTOR, BEST DIRECTOR, BEST SCREENPLAY. RATED R FOR LANGUAGE AND SEXUAL CONTENT.

The world is charged with the grandeur of God.
   –George Manley Hopkins

Finally, beloved, whatever is true, whatever is honorable, whatever is just, whatever is pure, whatever is pleasing, whatever is commendable, if there is any excellence and if there is anything worthy of praise, think about these things.
   –Philippians 4:8

Tips for Using This Movie

This is a funny, heartbreaking, and profound film about the power of beauty and the effect it can have on the heart that is open to it. The epilogue that ends the film is a stunning visual and verbal tribute to the daily gifts life holds out to us in abundance.

American Beauty is a complicated work of art that was showered with Oscars and awards from film critics in 1999. But it is not for those who are uncomfortable with strong language and controversial themes. It is an R-rated movie, perhaps less for the sexual content (although there is an almost-relationship between a middle-aged man and a teenager) than for the language. I have selected the scenes very carefully, but even in these scenes, there is a reference to masturbation as well as some profanity. Be sure to preview the scenes to assure that you—and the group—will be comfortable with the subject matter. You will have to make a judgment call on this. The movie is probably not appropriate for teenagers, which is unfortunate, because they would be among its most appreciative and receptive viewers.

Although this film is available on DVD, I have included VCR clips since more precise scene selection is possible and potentially objectionable material is kept to a minimum.

Many viewers need to watch this movie at least twice to see past some of the troubling themes to the deep, insightful, and profound gift this film offers. It is fairly easy to choose key scenes to focus on, leaving the rest for those who want to watch the film in its entirety. The scenes selected for use here are, in fact, excellent preparation to receive the whole movie as the work of art that it is.

This film examines themes of boredom, loneliness, and desperation in suburban America. It is wrenching in its honesty, and inspirational in the hope and perspective it offers. There is beauty in the most mundane aspects of life, the filmmakers say, and that is the comfort that God offers us: healing, there for the taking to mend our broken souls. You will want to replay it a second time, because every frame is powerful.

Background

To provide a context for the excerpts and to help participants follow the movie line, read this background information to the group.

American Beauty is the story of Lester Burnham, a forty-two-year-old advertising writer who initially describes himself as "dead." He's not sure what he's lost along the way but remembers, "I didn't always feel this sedated." He detests his job, has lost all connection with his wife and teenage daughter, and simply goes through the motions of living.

Lester's wife Carolyn cultivates a sterile, forced perfectionism as a real estate agent and as a homemaker. The table setting and background music for family dinners are more important to her than the interactions that take place there. She evaluates the American Beauty roses that she grows in the front yard (so they can be seen) with a critical eye, more interested in fertilizer and growing methods than in the loveliness of the blossoms. The color of her gardening clogs matches the color of her pruning sheers.

But perfectionism has its price. Carolyn sacrifices a loving relationship with her family as well as much of her integrity for appearances and gradually loses touch with reality and a sense of self. She seems to have sacrificed a lot for her lifestyle.

Lester is pronounced "expendable" at his job, but manages to leave the agency with a generous severance package because he knows about his boss's promiscuity. His new freedom not only invigorates Lester; it also brings the pain of his life into clearer focus. Shortly after losing his job, he becomes obsessed with Angela, a fifteen-year-old friend of his daughter. His thinly veiled lust obsesses him while, at the same time, it strangely brings him back to life. He makes tentative overtures to the girl, sometimes realizing how ridiculous he must seem and, at other times, confident that he has a chance with her.

Meanwhile, his daughter Janie is carrying on a serious relationship with the boy next door, who is anything but the wholesome, preppy stereotype. His is the truest voice in the film, because Ricky sees life through the eyes of the artist. While showing Janie a magical, lyrical sequence he videotaped of a plastic bag dancing in the wind, he confesses, "Sometimes there is so much beauty in the world, I feel like I can't take it. And my heart is going to cave in."

Lester and Carolyn's marriage continues to unravel as Lester struggles with his own journey to forge a new identity. It is a painful, erratic process and comes to a tragic end. But whatever qualms and discomfort the viewer has endured are more than redeemed with Lester's closing monologue, a tender and revelatory ode to beauty and its power to make even Lester overwhelmingly grateful for what he calls "my stupid little life."

Reflection: Caught Off-Guard

Read this selection to the group. Or, you may wish to use this reflection as a springboard to writing a reflection of your own to share with the group.

Wonder is a pause in reason.
  –Samuel Johnson

Several years ago I made my first trip to Paris. Like so many visitors, I immediately fell in love with the city and all things French. If it's true that we travel to discover a missing piece of ourselves, I found that piece here: the Angelina Tea Room, the gardens of the Tuilleries, the glory of the Paris Opera, even the exquisite lamp posts that border the boulevards.

One day we went to Musée d'Orsay, home of Impressionist masterpieces by the artists Monet, Renior, and Manet. As I walked through the exhibits and looked closely at these treasures, I had a startling reaction. Tears were streaming down my face and I was unable to stop them. Not only did I know that I was in the actual presence of genius, but deep feelings of love, understanding, and sympathy for all human beings washed over me. I knew these people in paint. The message in my mind reverberated: We're all the same. Human experience now and two hundred years ago—it's the same. Love is the same. Heartbreak is the same. Beauty is the same. We are all God's children, throughout the ages.

It was more than just a reaction to beautiful art that moved me. I was also hungering for something that I didn't know I was missing. As Joan Chittister puts it, "Beauty breaks open the human soul to what is possible in the face of the impossible . . . . Beauty is the spirituality of hope in the midst of alienation."[16]

American Beauty speaks directly to the "sedation" that we can feel in our lives, a feeling of being disconnected, numb, operating on "auto-pilot." A counterpoint to this state of mind is found in a legend about Siddhartha Gautama, the man eventually known as the Buddha. In their struggle to understand him, his followers ask him if he is a god or, perhaps, a saint. "No," the Buddha replied. "I am awake."

Intentionally seeking beauty can be a vehicle for spiritual growth. Thomas Moore writes, "Beauty is arresting. For the soul, it is important to be taken out of the rush of practical life for the contemplation of timeless and eternal realities."[17]

Beauty and art can also place a personal experience into a historical and religious context that give it meaning. Former public radio commentator Eric Friesen gives this account:

> On Good Friday, 1944, a distraught Bavarian nobleman sat at his writing desk in his ancestral family house just outside Munich. From the earliest days of National Socialism he had kept a scandalously candid and scathing daily account of life inside the Third Reich . . .
>
> On that Good Friday morning, late in World War II, Fritz Reck continued to chronicle the spiritual degradation of his country in his diary while listening to Bach's *St. Matthew Passion* on the radio. And then, as the final chorus begins with its unforgettable words: "*Wir setzen un mit tranen nieder*—in tears of grief, dear Lord, we leave Thee, Hearts cry out to Thee, May the sinner, worn with weeping, comfort find in thy dear keeping," he is swept up in the terrible irony of his own despair mirroring that of the faithful, grieving at the cross. The music releases his despair and at the same time, brings him the most profound consolation.[18]

Friesen calls this coincidence the "exquisite randomness" through which artistic expression can pierce an individual heart. And it is not only great art that can produce this reaction, but also the most commonplace and homely incidents: a glimpse of deep blue morning glories on a white trellis, a phone call that lifts you out of your depression, a warm greeting from a pet.

One strategy for instituting more contemplative discipline into our lives is to reinstitute a personal Sabbath, a restorative and healing time apart from the week's routine. Religious historian Huston Smith says that the greatest loss suffered by contemporary Christianity is the loss of the Sabbath. For many, if not most Americans, Sunday afternoons are just a day to catch up with tasks not completed the previous week or to get a head start on the next week's work. In Genesis, we learn that God "rested" on the seventh day, but perhaps God also used this time to contemplate and enjoy the beauty and goodness of creation. A personal Sabbath—which wouldn't even have to occur on Sundays—allows a space in our minds and hearts for all the things that constant activity blocks out, including the beauty of the everyday.

Following close behind grace-filled moments of beauty is a heart full of gratitude and a whispered prayer for the abundance of blessings that pervade our own "stupid little lives."

Film, Faith, and Scripture

Explore with your group the connections between film, faith, and Scripture by examining what the Bible says to us about our response to beauty. You may read the scripture passages from your book, or ask participants to look them up and read them to the group.

Jesus Expects Gratitude (Luke 17:11–19)

On the way to Jerusalem, Jesus was going through the region between Samaria and Galilee. As he entered a village, ten lepers approached him. Keeping their distance, they called out, saying, "Jesus, Master, have mercy on us!" When he saw them, he said to them, "Go and show yourself to the priests." And as they went, they were made clean. Then one of them, when he saw that he was healed, turned back, praising God with a loud voice. He prostrated himself at Jesus' feet and thanked him. And he was a Samaritan. Then Jesus asked, "Were not ten made clean? But the other nine, where are they? Was none of them found to return and give praise to God except this foreigner?" Then he said to him, "Get up and go on your way; your faith has made you well."

The Goodness of Creation (Genesis 1:31)

God saw everything that he had made, and indeed, it was very good.

The Lilies (Matthew 6:28–29)

"Consider the lilies of the field, how they grow; they neither toil nor spin, yet I tell you, even Solomon in all his glory was not clothed like one of these."

Film Clips to Use for a One-Hour Class
(Do not use DVD to show this film.)
Set VCR to zero at "Dreamworks."

1. (9 min.) Opening of film—Lester describes his life; we meet the Burnham family; Lester has a conversation with his boss; dinner at the Burnham's. End after Lester says to Janie, "We used to be pals."
   VCR—0:00 to 9:00
2. (6 min.) Janie converses with her neighbor Ricky; he shows her a videotape; family dinner the night after Lester loses his job. End after Lester's reference to Lawrence Welk.
   VCR—1:01:00 to 1:07:00
3. (2–5 min.) Lester has been killed by the next-door neighbor; begin scene as he is on the garage floor: "You always hear your entire life . . . ." Scenes of gratitude interspersed with people reacting to Lester's murder. Go to the end of the film.
   VCR—1:53:00 to 1:55:00 (or further if you want to listen to music underlying closing credits)

Total running time: 16–20 minutes

Discussion Questions

Invite participants to take a look at how the two texts—the film American Beauty *and the Bible—inform us, as people of faith, about the ways that beauty—and our awareness of it—brings us closer to God, deepens our faith, and enriches our lives.*

1. At the beginning of the film, what do you think accounts for Lester's unhappiness? Besides the dialogue we hear, what visual cues tell us about Lester's state of mind?
2. In a film, as in a work of art, assume that no detail is random. Why do you think the main character has been given his name? Discuss the implications of the name: Les-ter Burn-ham.
3. What does Carolyn's focus on success and perfectionism cut out of her life? Compare her attitude with the one Jesus recommends in Matthew 6:28–29.
4. If you had to compile a list, as Lester does at the end of the movie, of the beauty you have experienced in your life, what are

three or four things that would be on your list? The group
leader may want to write these things on a board or easel. Then
discuss if there is consensus about what the most indispensable
things of beauty are for people. Or is "necessary" beauty totally
subjective? These questions may help people answer the question above:
- What is an everyday object or thing that is beautiful because
  of the memories it holds for you? (Lester chooses the
  Firebird, his grandmother's hands, etc.).
- What was an experience that brought you a new understanding of the meaning of beauty? What did you learn?
- Why does someone in your life that you consider "beautiful"
  deserve that label?

5. The movie makes the point that beauty is a powerful motivation for thankfulness. How has an awareness of beauty transformed a moment for you and led you to prayer? What are the
   most powerful motivations for thankfulness?
6. Experiencing beauty is one thing that may inspire feelings of
   deep gratitude to God. But prayers of thanksgiving have many
   functions in addition to thanking God for blessings received.
   What are some of the other functions they serve?
7. What does the story of the ten lepers say about gratitude—in
   the actions of the leper who is thankful, as well as in the actions
   of the other nine? Specifically, what does it say about God's
   expectations about gratitude?

Extension Activity

Invite group members to bring a picture of "fleeting beauty" to the
next meeting and to write a short piece about how it relates to their
own attitudes towards change. Individually or as a group, explore the
fact that Jesus exhorts us to consider a thing (flower) whose beauty is
fleeting, here today and gone tomorrow. What does this tell us about
beauty? About life?

CHAPTER 10

Repentance: Why Is Confession Good for the Soul?

Dead Man Walking

Polygram Pictures, 1995, with Susan Sarandon, Sean Penn. Directed by Tim Robbins; nominated for four Academy Awards with Susan Sarandon winning as Best Actress; designated by over fifty film critics as one of the ten best films of the year. Rated R for some violent scenes.

Spiritual empowerment is evidenced in our lives by our willingness to tell ourselves the truth.[19]
   –Christina Baldwin, *Life's Companion*, 1991

Now I rejoice, not because you were grieved, but because your grief led to repentance.
   –2 Corinthians 7:9

Tips for Using This Movie

Do not be afraid of this film! It has dark elements, to be sure, but the clips here avoid most of the violent crime scenes. The scene at the end that leads up to Matthew Poncelet's death by lethal injection is extremely powerful and puts life and death issues literally in your face.

Be sure to end the last clip exactly where indicated, because what follows is a violent scene that may be upsetting to many, and hinder discussion as well.

Do not let the discussion become a debate about the pros and cons of capital punishment. Initially, the focus should be on the ideas of repentance, redemption, and ministry, although subsequent discussion could lead to a group study of capital punishment and Christianity.

You will see why this film was nominated for four Academy Awards—for its superb screenplay, haunting soundtrack by Bruce Springsteen, and riveting performances by Sean Penn and Susan Sarandon. There could not be a better film to launch a discussion about the power of repentance and about the ways we are called to serve one another.

Background

To provide a context for the excerpts and to help participants follow the movie line, read this background information to the group.

Dead Man Walking tells a story of redemption on death row in Angola Prison in Louisiana. It features a highly-acclaimed script adapted by director Tim Robbins from the autobiography of Helen Prejean, a nun of the Order of the Sisters of St. Joseph of Medaille. By the end of the movie, convicted killer Matthew Poncelet walks to his execution as the child of God he has come to believe he is, largely due to the ministry of Sister Helen.

Poncelet has been on death row for six years. Convicted of the murder of two teenagers and the rape of one, Poncelet initially maintains his innocence while trying to get his death sentence overturned by any means possible. Somehow, Poncelet gets the name of Sister Helen and writes to her, asking her to help him move his case forward more rapidly, since the date for his execution is growing closer.

Helen Prejean, living and working among the poor in the St. Thomas projects in New Orleans, has never even been in a prison before and is apprehensive when she receives Poncelet's letter. Their initial meeting is awkward and frustrating for both of them, but she commits to visiting Matthew regularly and "being present." He casts his lot with her because, he says, "Sister, you're all I've got."

As the legal efforts on his behalf flounder, Poncelet grows more desperate. Initially hostile, defensive, self-pitying, and bitter, he is resistant to Sister Helen's efforts to get him to face the truth about what happened the night of the murders. However, she is unwavering in her attempts to convince Poncelet to take ownership of his actions and to ask forgiveness from the victims' families and from God. It is that repentance, she believes, that will allow him to accept the love of God and to die with dignity.

A parallel story line concerns the victims' parents, the Perceys and the Delacourtes. The Perceys' daughter Hope was raped and murdered and the Delacourtes' son Walter killed after being attacked in an isolated lover's lane late at night. The families believe that Poncelet and his accomplice are, without doubt, guilty, and deserve to die. In their deep suffering and mourning for their beloved children, they are consumed by bitterness and hatred. Sister Helen tries to console both families, to no avail.

Hours before the scheduled execution, the last of the legal efforts fail and the governor refuses to overturn the sentence. The prison guard begins the procession to the death chamber with chilling words that echo through the cell block: "Dead man walking." Matthew Poncelet walks to his execution with Sister Helen at his side, reading from Isaiah: "Do not be afraid, I have redeemed you; I have called you by name, you are mine. When you pass through the waters, I will be with you; and through the rivers, they shall not overwhelm you; when you walk through the fire you will not be burned, and the flame will not consume you."

Before his death, Poncelet faces the Perceys and the Delacourtes and asks their forgiveness. Strapped down and about to die (in a position that resembles a crucifixion), he follows Sister Helen's instructions to "look at me when they do this thing to you. I will be the face of love for you."

Reflection: The Kiss

Read this selection to the group. Or, you may wish to use this reflection as a springboard to writing a reflection of our own to share with the group.

". . . and you will know the truth, and the truth will make you free."
    –John 8:32

There is a legend that in biblical times women used to collect their tears in small containers. The more tears you had, the closer you were to salvation. The underlying belief seems to be that the more deeply you allow yourself to experience the profound pain and rapturous joy of life—both occasions for tears—the closer you are to God. The legend also says that the woman who washed the feet of Jesus with her tears in the Book of Matthew poured out the contents of her tear jar, a lifetime of joys and sorrows, at the feet of Jesus.

So often, it seems, repentance is accompanied by tears.

As we inventory our personal failings, our inability to reach the standards we have set for ourselves or those we believe God sets for us, deep sadness may set in. As we remember the hurt we have caused other people, the selfishness that has dictated our actions—all in the face of the abundant blessings that pervade our lives—our hearts break and the tears flow.

Tears and the things that prompt them are important in the spiritual life. Clarissa Pinkola Estes writes: "Tears are a river that take you somewhere. Weeping creates a river around the boat that carries your soul-life. Tears lift your boat off the rocks, off dry ground, carrying it down river to someplace new, someplace better."[20]

Awareness of the depth and breadth of life experience surrounds sincere repentance. Along with the "amendment of life" that is the other half of the penitential act, these things can form an intense spiritual practice that promotes health and renewal. Joan Chittister observes, "The nice thing about guilt is that it proves we are still alive."[21] But we are also called to move from repentance to reconciliation and intentional care for one another. Consequently, *Dead Man Walking* not only focuses on the process of accountability and honesty to which Sister Helen leads Matthew Poncelet, it also illuminates the care, strength, and perseverance that goes into intense, personal ministry.

Bringing the news of the love of God to a cynical, hardcore prisoner on death row is a daunting task. Sister Helen says that Jesus taught that each person is worth more than his or her worst act, and this belief is what drives her, even when she is repulsed and horrified by Poncelet's actions. Ultimately, what Sister Helen leads Matthew to is the reality of God's love, even for him. It is almost too simple a proposition to put forth in such complex and depressing circumstances. Yet it is the only answer she has.

In Fyodor Dostoevski's classic story "The Grand Inquisitor" (in the novel *The Brothers Karamazov*), the Prisoner (who is Christ) is questioned by the Inquisitor, a cynical old man. He calls upon Jesus to explain the pain and injustice in the world. In sadistic detail, the Inquisitor describes the suffering of innocent children: the little girl of seven routinely beaten by her father; the boy of eight torn to pieces by the dogs of a sadistic general. The agony of these children proves to the Inquisitor the absurdity of the divinely created order of things. Page after page, the Inquisitor argues, harangues, and derides God, religion, and the church for their failings. Finally he pauses and waits for the Prisoner to respond to the charges.

There is a long period of silence, and still no reply from the Prisoner. The Inquisitor is frustrated and angry. He knows that the Prisoner has listened carefully and quietly to all of his rageful queries and charges. His patience is wearing thin.

And then the Inquisitor is given his answer. The Prisoner approaches him and softly kisses him on the lips. The conversation is over.[22]

And that is the answer God gives us as well. In Jesus. On the Cross. In the Resurrection. The divine kiss of love. It is our answer and our mandate.

All of us can find ourselves in *Dead Man Walking*: perhaps in the agony of the parents who have lost the people dearest to them; in the denial and rationalizations of Matthew Poncelet; or in the good intentions and dedicated, persevering ministry of Sister Helen. At various times in our lives, we may find ourselves in any one of these roles.

Jesus was not crucified alone. Various extremes of the human condition were represented on the two crosses on each side of him. On one side was the thief who derided Jesus and could not believe his preposterous claims. On the other side was the thief who had heard the message of Jesus and begged for reconciliation. And in the center—between these polarities of belief and disbelief, between faith and doubt, between our good intentions and failure to act, between the paradoxical opposites and competing tensions in which we live each day, is Jesus, arms outstretched, embracing all extremes of the human condition and the complexities of the human heart.

In one of her sermons, Barbara Brown Taylor put it this way: "There may be only one cross here today, but God knows we are all hanging on the other two. Whenever we stand near his, we complete the tableaux. One cross makes a crucifix. Three crosses make a church."[23]

Film Clips to Use for a One-Hour Class
Set VCR to zero at "Polygram Entertainment."

1. (8 min.) Sister Helen arrives at Angola Prison for the first meeting with Matthew Poncelet in response to a letter from him. First, she must be cleared by the prison chaplain. (This section also includes brief flashbacks to what Sister Helen imagines happened the night of the crime.) End after Poncelet says, "You've got guts . . . ."

    VCR—5:00 to 13:00   DVD—begin at Scene 2

2. (17 min.) Weeks have passed and all of Poncelet's options have run out. There will be no appeal; the lie detector test has been inconclusive. He continues to deny responsibility for the crime. Sister Helen visits Poncelet on the day of his execution. Following Poncelet's "last words," the execution takes place, Be sure to end this section right after the close-ups of the execution machine being turned on.

    VCR—1:30:00 to 1:47:00   DVD—begin at Scene 15

Total running time: 26 minutes

Film, Faith, and Scripture

Explore with your group the connections between film, faith, and Scripture by examining what the Bible says to us about repentance, forgiveness, and reconciliation. You may read the scripture passages from your book, or ask participants to look them up and read them to the group.

Repentance (Matthew 27:3)

When Judas, his betrayer, saw that Jesus was condemned, he repented and brought back the thirty pieces of silver to the chief priests and the elders.

Repent and Believe (Mark 1:14–15)

Now after John was arrested, Jesus came to Galilee, proclaiming the good news of God, and saying, "The time is fulfilled, and the kingdom of God has come near; repent, and believe in the good news."

Parable of the Lost Sheep (Luke 15:6–7)

"Rejoice with me, for I have found my sheep that was lost. Just so, I tell you, there will be more joy in heaven over one sinner who repents than over ninety-nine righteous persons who need no repentance."

Forgiveness and Repentance (Luke 17:3)

"If another disciple sins, you must rebuke the offender, and if there is repentance, you must forgive."

We Are Here to Serve Each Other (Hebrews 1:14)

Are not all angels spirits in the divine service, sent to serve for the sake of those who are to inherit salvation?

Remember Prisoners (Matthew 25:34–36, 40)

"Come, you that are blessed by my Father, inherit the kingdom prepared for you from the foundation of the world; for I was hungry and you gave me food, I was thirsty and you gave me something to drink, I was a stranger and you welcomed me, I was naked and you gave me clothing, I was sick and you took care of me, I was in prison and you visited me. . . . Truly I tell you, just as you did it to one of the least of these who are members of my family, you did it to me."

Discussion Questions

1. At first Matthew Poncelet rationalizes his behavior: no love as a child, the negative influence of his accomplice, being under the influence of drugs and alcohol. What inaccurate or even

dishonest messages do you send to yourself about your own behavior? Why is honesty a condition for reconciliation?

2. Sister Helen's response that much of what she does is not faith, "it's work," speaks to a necessary discipline often present in the religious life. What is something that you do to reach out and help others that feels more like work than like an expression of faith? What, if anything, is the reward in such an experience?

3. What about forgiveness? Has the act of forgiveness ever felt more like work than faith to you? Give an example.

4. Rabbi Kushner states, "The ability to love and the ability to forgive are weapons that God has given us to live fully in this less-than-perfect world."[24] Describe a time when you used love as a survival skill. What is a time when you used forgiveness as a survival skill?

5. Could you forgive Poncelet if you were the Perceys or the Delacourtes? What is the alternative to forgiveness?

6. What was your reaction to the scene at the end where Poncelet says his final words? Are there any forces that you believe have "crucified" Poncelet?

Extension Activities

Write a reflection on one of the following questions in your journal or share your responses in a small group.

1. Sister Helen says, "There are places of sorrow only God can touch." Where might be some of those places in the world today? In your own heart?

2. When have you asked another person to forgive you? What prompted you to do so? What was the result?

3. Read Helen Prejean's account of her experience at Angola in her book *Dead Man Walking: An Eyewitness Account of the Death Penalty in the United States* (Vintage Books, 1996).

CHAPTER 11

Acceptance: What Is the Difference Between Accepting and "Settling"?

The Prince of Tides

COLUMBIA PICTURES, 1991, WITH NICK NOLTE, BARBRA STREISAND, BLYTHE DANNER. DIRECTED BY BARBRA STREISAND; NOMINATED FOR SEVEN ACADEMY AWARDS. RATED R.

Happy families are all alike; every unhappy family is unhappy in its own way.
–Leo Tolstoy, *Anna Karenina,* 1875.

Tips for Using This Movie

Part of the appeal of this movie is the heart-wrenching beauty of its beginning and the profound questions raised by its ending. The scenes selected represent only one story line from the film, so that the discussion can be clearly focused on the theme of self-acceptance. The other story lines are discussed in the following section for background purposes.

People who want to watch the movie in its entirety should know that there is a violent, disturbing rape scene in the middle of the film. It is hard to watch, to say the least, but is central to the story. Also, be aware that each of the three main characters has an extramarital affair, although this is not dealt with explicitly in the clips selected.

The relationship between Tom Wingo (Nick Nolte), a high school teacher and football coach, and Susan Lowenstein (Barbra Streisand), the psychiatrist who is working with Tom's suicidal sister and helps Tom finally deal with his destructive memories, is downplayed in the selected clips. Viewers should be informed, however, that it is Lowenstein's name that is referenced as Tom drives across the bridge in Charleston at the end of the movie.

You may want to play the ending segment twice, since each line of dialogue presents a provocative theme of its own.

Background

To provide a context for the excerpts and to help participants follow the movie line, read this background information to the group.

Even before the credits, the film opens with scenes of lush seascapes, bathed in beauty.

We see radiant images of the South Carolina coast, its islands and inlets, and the luminous, golden sea, as we hear the thick, honeyed voice of the main character, Tom Wingo, describe a childhood that was a complete contradiction to this natural grandeur. He tells us, "There are families who live out their entire lives without a single thing of interest happening to them. I've always envied those families."

Tom is one of three children of a harsh, violent father who runs a shrimp boat and a self-protective, ruthless, beautiful mother. During the many tortured times at home, when their father is drinking and abusive and their mother combative, the three children find their only escape in jumping off the dock into the sea, taking refuge in its underwater sanctuary. They hold hands under water, forming a tenuous family circle, and stay there until their lungs force them back to the surface and to the reality of their troubled home.

Following Tom's introductory monologue and the opening credits, the main action of the story begins at the seaside home of the middle-aged Tom, a high school English teacher and football coach, his wife Sally, a physician, and their three young daughters. Tom, haunted by his past, has become distant with Sally, especially since the death of his older brother Luke two years earlier. His emotional distance and his dissatisfaction with his job and his life, amplified by his mother's criticism, have left Sally feeling confused, angry, and hurt.

Lila, Tom's mother, arrives one afternoon to announce that Tom's sister Savannah has again attempted suicide. Preoccupied with planning a birthday celebration for her second husband and not likely to be welcomed by Savannah anyway, Lila asks Tom to go to New York to help his sister.

Arriving in New York, he moves into Savannah's empty apartment and visits her in the hospital's psychiatric unit, where she is sedated but pleased to see him. Tom becomes involved with her psychiatrist, Susan Lowenstein, at first to discuss Savannah, later to confront his own family issues, and finally, as a lover. He starts coaching her son Bernard, a budding musician and an aspiring football player. He is invited to a party at Susan's home and is humiliated by her husband, a world-renowned musician and arrogant sophisticate.

Ultimately, Tom and Susan's brief affair ends and Tom goes back to Sally, healed of his childhood pain and confident and accepting of who he is and what he does. Tom has always been a thoughtful man, but is especially so after these experiences, acknowledging, "It is the mystery of life that sustains me now."

Reflection: The Peace

Read this selection to the group. Or, you may wish to use this reflection as a springboard to writing a reflection of your own to share with the group.

You can't achieve peace by avoiding life.
    –Virginia Woolf

After a ten-year absence from church, I became an Episcopalian in my late twenties. Still bearing scars from a fundamentalist Lutheran upbringing, I was wary, but yielded to parental pressure to have my daughters baptized. I was pleasantly surprised—and relieved—to find an Episcopal church with a liberal theology and intriguing liturgy. Since the rector would not baptize our children until my husband and I became part of the community, we went to classes, made friends, and found ourselves at home.

One liturgical practice, however, made my skin crawl: the congregation passing the peace in the middle of the service. Writer Garrison Keillor is absolutely correct in his observation that Scandinavian

Lutherans (myself included) can be a cold bunch! I was not accustomed to touching people in church—not even shaking hands, and certainly not hugging. In my parents' home, affection was never, never displayed physically. No good-bye or hello hugs, no comradely arm around the shoulder; we each existed in our independent shells. The Peace made me so uncomfortable that I would often pretend my baby was fussing and I had to take her out of the sanctuary during this time, just to escape.

Of course, patterns break, times change, and growth comes. The Peace is no longer a problem for me, but I continue to hold my now-deceased parents accountable for withholding physical (and often verbal) affection from my brother and me. I insist it is their fault that our family was not like the warm, physically-expressive Italian families that I knew. As an adult, I have chosen to try to learn new ways of relating to other human beings (including hugging!) but even today, physical affection seems to be more difficult for me than for many others.

Of course, I recognize that my mom and dad learned their patterns from the families they grew up in, and from their own parents. They were not naturally cold and uncaring people; in fact, I've grown to admire their reserve and dignity. I have, however, tried to break the cycle by showering my own kids with physical affection.

Blaming our parents for an imperfect upbringing is commonplace, and coming to terms with blaming them can be an important part of work in therapy. Tom Wingo is a different person altogether when he is able to talk through and then let go of what his parents did to their family, and then stop seeing his entire reality through this lens.

Not only do we confront the idiosyncrasies and potential damaging effects of our upbringing on our path to self-acceptance, we address the challenges and obstacles that life hands us. As stages of our lives unfold, we have to decide if we will accept them, fight them, or let go and move through them. Letting go is immensely difficult for some of us, even if we know it's the wisest course. A friend once told me, "I've never let go of anything I haven't left claw marks on."

There is also tremendous societal pressure that affects our ability to accept who we are and the paths our lives take. We are vulnerable to pressures to be financially and professionally successful and to have an ideal family, a cadre of close friends, and a comfortable home. When do we push for more on these fronts—and when do we settle for what we have?

But perhaps "settling" is merely thoughtful acceptance. Like Tom, I am a high school teacher, and have had a lifelong battle with myself about the worth of what I do—high school teaching, after all, doesn't bring status or wealth. Tom's mother is disappointed that, given his abilities, he isn't doing more with his life, and I have had similar experiences. The scene at the party where Susan's husband ridicules Tom's career is a painful example of this attitude. Yet ultimately Tom is able to acknowledge his choice of career as a good one, consistent with who he really is. It was not "settling" for him; it was acknowledgment of where his talents, passions, and interests lay.

The Prince of Tides dramatizes the movement from self-doubt to self-acceptance and then to the next step: openness to what Tom calls "the mystery of life." That mystery becomes the sustaining force in his life. It can be the sustaining force in our lives, too.

Clips for a One-Hour Class
Set VCR on zero at "Columbia Pictures."

1. (12 min.) The beginning of the movie (pre-credits); Tom recounts his troubled childhood. The adult Tom and his wife Sally discuss their troubled marriage while walking on the beach. End after Tom's run on the beach.
   VCR—00:00 to 12:00   DVD—begin at Scene 1

2. (7 min.) Susan's husband Herbert is playing the violin. Tom attends a dinner party at the apartment of Lowenstein and her famous musician husband. He has been staying in New York to be near his sister Savannah (who has again attempted suicide). He has grown closer to Susan Lowenstein as she has helped him come to terms with his troubled past. He has also been teaching her son to play football. End after Tom leaves the party.
   VCR—1:41:00 to 1:48:00   DVD—begin at Scene 23

3. (4 min.) City lights; Tom bids good-bye to Lowenstein after their brief affair. He is reconciling with his wife Sally. Tom returns home to Charleston and his family and makes peace with his life. Continue until "the end."
   VCR—2:03:00 to end   DVD—begin at Scene 27

Total running time: 23 minutes

Film, Faith, and Scripture

Explore with your group the connections between film, faith, and Scripture by examining what the Bible says to us about accept-ance and ambition. You may read the scripture passages from your book, or ask participants to look them up and read them to the group.

Moses Claims He's Unworthy of Leadership (Exodus 4:10–13)

But Moses said to the Lord, "O my Lord, I have never been eloquent, neither in the past nor even now that you have spoken to your servant; but I am slow of speech and slow of tongue." Then the Lord said to him, "Who gives speech to mortals? Who makes them mute or deaf, seeing or blind? Is it not I, the Lord? Now go, and I will be with your mouth and teach you what you are to speak." But he said, "O my Lord, please send someone else."

Gifts and Abilities Given to All (1 Corinthians 7:7)

But each has a particular gift from God, one having one kind and another a different kind.

Attend to Your Gifts (1 Timothy 4:14)

Do not neglect the gift that is in you . . . .

Discussion Questions

1. At what times in your life have you "settled" for something instead of continuing a search for something better? What led to your decision? What have been the results?
2. In what areas of your life do you want to make progress before you are willing to accept them as the way they will be indefi-nitely? A relationship? A job? Pursuing your talents or dreams?

How much of this do you think is a part of our can-do, self-help American culture? How much do you think is rooted in the human condition?

3. (The leader may ask the group to reflect on these questions silently, allowing ample time after each one, and then invite members to share with the group what they choose.) At the end of the film, Tom Wingo pays tribute to the psychiatrist who helped him to heal—and whom he has loved—by repeating her name several times. Whose name would you repeat "as prayer, as praise, as regret" for the difference he or she has made in your life?
   - What would be your prayer for him or her?
   - Why would you praise him or her?
   - Is there an element of regret? If so, how would you describe it?

4. Tom says that he wishes that each of us were apportioned two lives instead of one. If you were given a second life, imagine what it might be like. What things would this second life have that your present life does not? What would you do in the second life that you haven't done in the present?

5. Tom concludes that he is "a teacher, a coach, and a well-loved man. And it is enough." Think about the gifts you have received from God and rewrite his statement, using three terms to describe the core of who you are. Can you, too, say that this is "enough"?

6. What is the problem Moses has in answering God's call to him? Why does he have difficulty acknowledging—and trusting in—the gifts God has endowed him with? Who are other biblical figures that struggle with self-worth or with an unsatisfactory life situation?

Extension Activities

Write in your journal and share with the group as you wish:

1. The Wingos are an exceptionally weird family by anyone's standards, but every single family has its own idiosyncrasies. Describe one incident that happened in your family during

your childhood or youth that you have had a hard time accepting. This could be something that you witnessed or that happened directly to you. Why was it so difficult to "accept"? How did you come to terms with it (if you did)?

2. Have there been any things or times or people in your life that (as Tom says) you choose not to remember? Explain.

CHAPTER 12

Empathy: How Is Empathy the Heart of Christian Faith?

To Kill a Mockingbird

UNIVERSAL PICTURES, 1962, WITH GREGORY PECK, MARY BADHAM, ROBERT DUVALL. DIRECTED BY ROBERT MULLIGAN; NOMINATED FOR EIGHT ACADEMY AWARDS, WINNING FOR BEST ACTOR, BEST ADAPTED SCREENPLAY, BEST ART AND SET DIRECTION. NOT RATED BUT SUITABLE FOR ALL AGES.

We want people to feel with us more than to act for us.
   –George Eliot

. . . and He had compassion for them . . . .
   –Mark 6:34

Tips for Using This Movie

Many people are familiar with the novel *To Kill a Mockingbird* since it has been a popular choice for high school English classes for forty years. Nearly everyone will welcome revisiting it, since this gently told story possesses tremendous power and beauty.

Viewers may be interested in some little-known facts about the movie. One is that the distinguished actor Gregory Peck (who received an Oscar for this role) says that this film was the high point of his career and that he never loved portraying any character as much as the lawyer Atticus Finch. This film also marks the film debut of acclaimed actor Robert Duvall, and the first Academy Award for screenwriter Horton Foote, who also won the award later for *Tender Mercies.*

Remind viewers that *To Kill a Mockingbird* was filmed in 1962 and will look different from the high-tech extravaganzas so popular today. For one thing, it is in black and white, not color. In actuality, this lends an aura of historical authenticity, since the story takes place during the Depression. Viewers will also notice that the pace of the film is slower than they are accustomed to; each shot seems to be longer, the editing is not as fast paced, and there is a forthright simplicity to the presentation.

Teenagers may find the cinematic style dated and slow moving, but if they can get by that, are certain to find the story engaging. Most adults will be captivated immediately and deeply affected by the eloquent conclusion, which allows us to understand the old adage of "walking around in someone else's skin" in a fresh and memorable way.

The scenes selected include the credits, which are important in setting the stage and establishing the tone for the story. Play all the clips, also using the transitional comments, before beginning the discussion.

NOTE: This film is not yet available on DVD.

Background

To provide a context for the excerpts and to help participants follow the movie line, read this background information to the group.

Based on the 1960 Pulitzer Prize–winning novel of the same name, *To Kill a Mockingbird* is the semi-autobiographical account of author Harper Lee's childhood in Monroeville, Alabama, called "Maycomb" in the film. It is the only book she wrote that enjoyed wide success.

The opening credits set the scene. We hear a few simple bars of piano music and then a child's voice humming as we see her small hand sorting through a cigar box full of trinkets: an old watch, a pocket knife, some marbles. Later we learn the significance of these treasures.

The story is set in the 1930s in a small, quiet Southern town. The author's words, taken for the most part directly from the book, provide the narration for the film. Immediately after the credits, the setting for the story is described in languorous, poetic language: "Maycomb was a tired old town, even in 1932 when I first knew it. Somehow it was hotter then. Ladies bathed in the morning, and after their three o'clock naps . . . ."

The plot focuses on two siblings: Jem, age ten, and Scout (Jean Louise), six. They live with their widowed father, Atticus Finch, a small-town lawyer known for his integrity and legal skills. The family's interactions with several individuals who are at once troubled and troubling form the basic plot lines over the course of two years.

One of these story lines involves Atticus's defense of a black man, Tom Robinson, on charges that he raped Mayella Ewell, the oldest daughter of a desperate, mean, drunken father. The other involves the Radley family, notably Arthur Radley, called "Boo" by the neighborhood children, who believe the rumors and gossip about him and envision Boo as a dangerous monster.

Behind these fanciful stories is something that happened when Boo was a teenager. He and some friends borrowed a car for a joyride, were arrested, and then locked in the courthouse basement. Mr. Radley eventually brought Boo home and, the story goes, "locked him away" in the house. Boo hasn't been seen since, giving rise to the scary tales about Boo that the children have created and embellished.

The clips chosen here involve the Radley story only, but its theme and moral is the same as in the Tom Robinson subplot in which Tom is victimized by the strong racial prejudice in Maycomb. The theme is also reflected in the story of a minor character, Mrs. DuBois, a notoriously mean, elderly neighbor who suffers great physical pain, yet battles to overcome her dependence on morphine before she dies. But she is also misunderstood and rejected by the community.

Yet all three of these characters bring gifts to the community. Mrs. DuBois is wretched and complaining, but beautifies Maycomb with the flowers in her front yard. Tom Robinson helps the tragic Mayella, whose father beats her. Boo Radley proves to be the guardian angel of Jem and Scout. They are all examples of Atticus's lesson to Scout that to harm the defenseless, especially those who "make beautiful music," is like shooting a harmless songbird. It's like killing a mockingbird.

Reflection: So Am I

Read this selection to the group. Or, you may wish to use this reflection as a springboard to writing a reflection of your own to share with the group.

At the very heart of Christian faith—the Incarnation of God in Jesus—is the concept of empathy.

God in Jesus became one of us and experienced the tribulations, suffering, and death we all face. He walked among us, experienced life as we know it, and in so doing, bridged the gulf between Earth and heaven.

From this comes his commandment to us, his followers, to do the same for each other, to have empathy for those on the journey with us. This goes beyond just helping them out to "getting inside their skin," as Atticus tells Scout, to help them from an informed position. Instead of asking, "What do you need?" we are first called to ask, "What are you going through?"

Several years ago, *Life* magazine reported a story of a ten-year-old boy in Indiana who underwent a series of chemotherapy treatments for cancer. His closest friends, his baseball teammates, were especially scared and worried. They were warned that when Billy returned to school, he'd be noticeably thinner and would have lost his hair. Eight weeks later, when Billy came back to school, he was greeted by a baseball team of sixth-grade boys—who had all had their heads shaved.

While empathy—feeling with others—and compassion are central aspects of the Christian journey, they are now more critical than ever if humankind is to continue to exist. Matthew Fox warns, "Now that the world is a global village, we need compassion more than ever— not for altruism's sake, nor for philosophy's sake or theology's sake, but for survival's sake."[25]

Gerda Weissmann Klein is a Holocaust survivor who has dedicated her life to telling her story, a story whose climax is a profound experience of empathy. She speaks to college, high school, civic, and religious groups, and has written the book *All but My Life,* the basis of an Academy Award-winning documentary by Kary Antholis.

Gerda Weissmann was a fifteen-year-old student in Poland when her Jewish family was deported to Auschwitz where her mother, father, and sister perished. There Gerda befriended Hilda, a girl her age, who died in her new friend's arms. Hilda's last words to Gerda were a request: "Promise me you'll hang on for one more week."

One week to the day later, after a horrible enforced march through the snow that killed all but 150 of the 2,000 girls at the camp, liberation came. Hilda had unwittingly given Gerda the gift of life by securing her promise to hang on for one more week. That day, the German guards and soldiers disappeared, and Gerda and another girl staggered in to the closest village. They were in rags, mere skeletons, and had not had a bath for three years.

There were many cars on the streets bearing American flags. One car pulled up to them, and an American soldier got out and beckoned them. Immediately, Gerda called out the standard warning, "Be careful! We're Jewish." In German, the soldier replied, "So am I." She recalls, "He held the door open for me, and in that simple gesture restored me to humanity." She describes this as the single greatest moment of her life. They later married and have been married for over fifty years.

Gerda Klein's message now is not to be afraid to face life because, if the worst happens, we have more resources than we know, more resilience than we can imagine. She notes that "evil" spelled backwards is "live."[26]

Empathy can conquer fear and open the door to understanding. At the end of *To Kill a Mockingbird*, Boo Radley stands by Jem's bed. Jem is still unconscious from injuries suffered when Bob Ewell attacked Jem and Scout the night they walked home from school after the Halloween pageant. Boo knows all too well what it's like to be hurt and victimized, as Jem has been that night. Silently, without a word, Boo extends his hand, touches Jem on the forehead, and then holds his hand over Jem in an unmistakable gesture of blessing and brotherhood.

Film, Faith, and Scripture

Explore with your group the connections between film, faith, and Scripture by examining what the Bible says to us about the centrality of empathy to our Christian faith. You may read the scripture passages from your book, or ask participants to look them up and read them to the group.

Jesus Calls for Empathy for the Adulteress (John 8:3–9)

The scribes and the Pharisees brought a woman who had been caught in adultery; and making her stand before all of them, they said to him, "Teacher, this woman was caught in the very act of committing adultery. Now in the law Moses commanded us to stone such women. Now what do you say?" . . . he straightened up and said to them, "Let anyone among you who is without sin be the first to throw a stone at her." . . . When they heard it, they went away . . . .

Jesus Has Compassion for the Suffering (Psalm 147:2–3)

The LORD builds up Jerusalem; he gathers the outcasts of Israel. He heals the brokenhearted, and binds up their wounds.

Outcasts Will Be Restored (Jeremiah 30:17)

"For I will restore health to you, and your wounds I will heal," says the Lord, "because they have called you an outcast."

The Compassion of Jesus (Mark 6:34)

As he went ashore, he saw a great crowd; and he had compassion for them, because they were like sheep without a shepherd; and he began to teach them many things.

Jesus Understands Human Weakness (Hebrews 4:14–15)

Since, then, we have a great high priest who has passed through the heavens, Jesus, the Son of God, let us hold fast to our confession. For we do not have a high priest who is unable to sympathize with our weaknesses, but we have one who in every respect has been tested as we are, yet without sin.

Clips to Use for a One-Hour Class

NOTE: This film is not yet available on DVD
Set VCR to zero at "Universal Pictures."

1. (11 min.) Credits; background on Maycomb; Mr. Cunningham's "entailment." Scout and Atticus argue. Jem and Scout tell their friend Dill about Boo Radley; Miss Stephanie relates more gossip about Boo. End after exterior shot of Radley house.
   VCR—0:00 to 11:00
2. (18 min.) Someone has left Jem and Scout a series of presents in the hollow of an oak tree in front of the Radley's before Mr. Nathan Radley cements the hole shut. Atticus is defending Tom Robinson against the charge that he raped Mayella Ewell;

Mr. Ewell has threatened the Finch family. Scene begins the night of the Halloween pageant, which is showcasing Maycomb's agricultural products; Scout is dressed as a ham! Walking home after the pageant, Scout and Jem are chased and attacked and later meet the one who rescued them. Go to end of film.

VCR—1:50:00 to end

Total viewing time: approximately 29 minutes

Discussion Questions

1. Who are some individuals (or groups of people) that you personally would have the most difficulty approaching with empathy and compassion? Why?
2. The term "outcasts" is used often in Scripture. Who are some famous biblical outcasts? Which groups of people (or individuals) are considered outcasts today?
3. Choose one specific person from question two. Suppose you had to find some common ground with this individual. How would you figure out what do to? From what sources would you seek inspiration or information? What basic human similarities or experiences between that person and yourself could you draw on?
4. What would you say is the essence of Jesus' teaching on how we should regard those different from ourselves? Who are those that Jesus does condemn?
5. Do you agree with the statement that the heart of Christian faith is the concept of empathy? Why or why not? Attempt to articulate what it is that most attracts you to Christianity.

Extension Activities

1. In your journal, write about a time when you felt like an outcast. What was the situation? How did you feel? How was the situation resolved?
2. Read the book *All but My Life* by Gerda Weissmann Klein (Hill & Wang, 1995).

NOTES

1. Albert Einstein, autobiographical handwritten note appearing in Ralph E. Lapp, "The Einstein Letter That Started It All," in the *New York Times Magazine*, August 2, 1964.

2. Huston Smith, "Another World to Live By," in *Teaching the Introductory Course in Religious Studies*, ed. Mark Juergensmayer (New York: Scholars Press, 1991).

3. Frederick Buechner, *The Alphabet of Grace* (New York: Seabury Press, 1970), 76.

4. Matthew Fox, *The Coming of the Cosmic Christ* (San Francisco: Harper & Row, 1988), 32.

5. Richard Llewellyn, *How Green Was My Valley* (New York: Laurel Publishing, 1940), 297.

6. M. Scott Peck, *The Road Less Traveled* (New York: Simon & Schuster, 1978), 15.

7. Parker Palmer, "Address to the Trinity Institute"(New York, 1994).

8. Bill Holm, *Prairie Days* (San Francisco: Saybrook Publishing, 1985), 59.

9. Mary Catherine Bateson, *Composing a Life* (New York: Atlantic Monthly Press, 1989), 9.

10. Lorene Carey, *Black Ice* (New York: Alfred A. Knopf, 1991), 218.

11. Philip Yancey, *Where Is God When It Hurts?* (Grand Rapids: Zondervan, 1990), 225–26.

12. Dick Lourie, *Ghost Radio* (Brooklyn, N.Y.: Hanging Loose Press, 1988).

13. The Book of Common Prayer (New York: Seabury Press, 1979), 42.

14. Cecil Murray, interview with Hugh Hewitt, "Searching for God in America," Community Television of California, 1996.

15. Joan Chittister, *In Search of Belief* (Ligiori, MO: Ligouri/Triumph Publications, 1999), 185.

16. Joan Chittister, *Living Well* (New York: Orbis, 2000), 14–15.

17. Thomas Moore, *Care of the Soul* (New York: HarperCollins, 1992), 278.

18. Eric Friesen, "Beneficiaries of an Exquisite Randomness," *Minneapolis Star-Tribune*, April 14, 1995.

19. Christina Baldwin, *Life's Companion: Journal Writing as a Personal Quest* (New York: Bantam, 1991).

20. Clarisa Pinkola Estes, *Women Who Run with the Wolves* (New York: Ballantine, 1992), 374.

21. Chittister, *In Search of Belief*, 157.

22. Fyodor Dostoevski, *The Brothers Karamazov* (1880; New York: Farrar, Straus & Giroux, 1990), 262

23. Barbara Brown Taylor, "The Man in the Middle," in *Home by Another Way* (Cambridge, MA: Cowley, 1999), 90.

24. Harold Kushner, *When Bad Things Happen to Good People* (New York: Shocken Books, 1997), 148.

25. Matthew Fox, *A Spirituality Named Compassion* (Minneapolis: Winston Press, 1979), i.

26. Gerda Weissman Klein, speech to students at the Blake School, Minneapolis, September 1999.